The Hands That Built This

Restoring Respect and Rebuilding the Future of the Trades

K. A. Pierce

© Copyright 2025 - All rights reserved.

The content contained within this book may not be reproduced, duplicated or transmitted without direct written permission from the author or the publisher.

Under no circumstances will any blame or legal responsibility be held against the publisher, or author, for any damages, reparation, or monetary loss due to the information contained within this book, either directly or indirectly.

Legal Notice:

This book is copyright protected. It is only for personal use. You cannot amend, distribute, sell, use, quote or paraphrase any part, or the content within this book, without the consent of the author or publisher.

Disclaimer Notice:

Please note the information contained within this document is for educational and entertainment purposes only. All effort has been executed to present accurate, up to date, reliable, complete information. No warranties of any kind are declared or implied. Readers acknowledge that the author is not engaged in the rendering of legal, financial, medical or professional advice. The content within this book has been derived from various sources. Please consult a licensed professional before attempting any techniques outlined in this book.

By reading this document, the reader agrees that under no circumstances is the author responsible for any losses, direct or indirect, that are incurred as a result of the use of the information contained within this document, including, but not limited to, errors, omissions, or inaccuracies.

Acknowledgments

This book could not have been built without the many voices, hands, and hearts that inspired it.

To the ironworkers, carpenters, welders, pipe fitters, electricians, and laborers I've worked alongside, thank you for your grit, wisdom, and stories. You were my first teachers, and your example lives in every chapter.

To the women in the trades—past, present, and rising—you carry more than tools. You carry hope. Thank you for your courage, sisterhood, and strength.

To the mentors who didn't just teach skills but showed what it means to have pride in your work, you shaped more than careers; you shaped character.

To the families who stand behind every *tradesperson*—who wait through late shifts, unpredictable hours, and the physical toll—thank you for being the quiet foundation beneath it all.

To the readers: Thank you for showing up. Whether you work with your hands or are just learning to, this story is yours now, too.

And to those we've lost along the way, your memory builds on in us.

With deep respect,

K. A. Pierce

Dedication

For the hands that shaped steel, laid brick, pulled wire, poured concrete, and never asked for applause... this is for you.

For the women who forged the way... this is for you.

For the mentors who taught without ego, the workers who gave without complaint, and the families who waited at home... this is for you.

For those we lost on the job... and the ones who carry their memory forward in every building and foundation... this is for you.

And for the next generation, may you build with pride, work with honor, and know you were never second best... this is for you.

To my dad, who had *skills* and could build or fix anything... this is for you, RIP.

To my brother, who carries on the Legacy with *skills* learned from Dad... this is for you.

Table of Contents

INTRODUCTION: NOT A BACKUP PLAN 1
    THE SHIFT IS COMING 2
    MORE THAN WORK: A WAY OF LIFE 3
    BREAKING THE CYCLE 4
    THE FOUNDATION WE STAND ON 4

CHAPTER 1: BUILT, NOT A BACKUP PLAN 7
    THE FIRST CHOICE THAT NO ONE TALKS ABOUT 7
    DEBT-FREE AND IN DEMAND 8
    REALITY CHECK: VALUE ISN'T ALWAYS FOUND IN A DEGREE 9
    THE SKILLS GAP REALITY 10
    BUILT BY CHOICE, NOT DEFAULT 10
    THE INTELLIGENCE OF THE HANDS 11
    MORE THAN A JOB—A WAY OF BEING 11

CHAPTER 2: THE LOST RESPECT FOR THE TRADES 13
    A CULTURE THAT FORGOT ITS BUILDERS 13
    THE PERVASIVE STIGMA 14
    REALITY CHECK: A GENERATION RAISED ON SCREENS 15
    THE PRESTIGE TRAP 16
    THE DANGEROUS CONSEQUENCES 17
    THE RESPECT DEFICIT 18
    RECLAIMING RESPECT 19
    THE PATH FORWARD 20

CHAPTER 3: WOMEN WHO WELD—SISTERHOOD IN STEEL 21
    NOT JUST A MAN'S WORLD 21
    THE DATA BEHIND THE DRIVE 22
    THE HARD AND THE HONEST 23
    BREAKING DOWN BARRIERS THROUGH TECHNOLOGY AND INNOVATION 24
    SISTERHOOD IN STEEL 25
    RISING THROUGH THE RANKS 28
    MENTORSHIP MATTERS 28
        Women in World War II 29
    REALITY CHECK: IF SHE CAN'T SEE IT, SHE CAN'T BE IT 30
    THE ECONOMIC IMPERATIVE 30
    THE PATH FORWARD 31
    OUR LEGACY 31

CHAPTER 4: FROM HARD SELL TO HARD HAT—RETHINKING RECRUITMENT ... 33

When Did We Stop Showing the Trades? ... 33
The Tide Is Turning ... 34
The Digital Natives Discover the Trades ... 35
Marketing That Misses the Mark ... 36
Reality Check: We're Not Just Competing With College ... 37
Cracking the Gen Z Code ... 37
   Platform-Specific Approaches ... *38*
   Content That Resonates ... *38*
Start With Exposure ... 39
   Early Engagement Strategies ... *39*
Building Authentic Employer Brands ... 39
   Key Elements of Authentic Trades Branding ... *40*
The Role of Technology in Modern Recruitment ... 40
   Targeted Digital Advertising ... *41*
   Multi-Channel Approach ... *41*
Measuring Success and Adapting ... 41
   Continuous Monitoring ... *42*
   Adaptation and Innovation ... *42*
We're Not Just Building Things; We're Building Awareness ... 42

CHAPTER 5: CRAFT, HONOR, AND PURPOSE ... 45

Craftsmanship Is a Calling ... 45
Honor in the Work ... 46
Reality Check: When the World Shut Down, the Trades Didn't ... 47
The Ultimate Test: September 11, 2001 ... 48
The Health Cost of Heroism ... 50
What You Build Builds You ... 50
A Legacy of Service ... 51
Recognition and Respect ... 52
The Continuing Call ... 52

CHAPTER 6: SKILLS THAT AREN'T LEARNED IN AN OFFICE ... 55

Learning on the Home Front ... 55
The Value of *Old School* Knowledge ... 56
The Great Knowledge Crisis ... 57
The Mentorship Solution ... 58
The Apprenticeship Model ... 59
A New Kind of Apprenticeship ... 60
Challenges in Knowledge Transfer ... 62
Modern Solutions for Ancient Wisdom ... 62
Reality Check: We've Outsourced Too Much ... 63
The Role of Technology in Knowledge Transfer ... 64

BUILDING A CULTURE OF KNOWLEDGE SHARING 65
MENTORSHIP ISN'T JUST FOR THE UNION HALL 65
THE MULTIGENERATIONAL OPPORTUNITY 66
THE FUTURE OF SKILLED LEARNING 67
PERSONAL RESPONSIBILITY 67

CHAPTER 7: DANGER, RISK, AND PRIDE—THE MENTAL WEIGHT OF THE TRADES 69

IT'S NOT JUST HARD WORK; IT'S HAZARDOUS WORK 69
    The Main Killer 70
THE SILENT EPIDEMIC: MENTAL HEALTH IN CONSTRUCTION 71
UNDERSTANDING THE RISK FACTORS 72
    Demographic Factors 73
    Cultural Factors 73
    Work-Related Stressors 73
    Physical Health Impacts 74
    Substance Use Issues 74
THE COMPOUND EFFECT 74
WARNING SIGNS AND RECOGNITION 75
    Behavioral Changes 75
    Physical Signs 75
    Emotional Indicators 76
BREAKING THE SILENCE 76
REALITY CHECK: ASKING FOR HELP ISN'T WEAKNESS 77
    Additional Resources 78
THE PATH FORWARD 78
RISK MEETS REWARD 79
BUILDING A CULTURE OF CARE 79

CHAPTER 8: FIXING THE PIPELINE—SCHOOLS, PARENTS, AND POLICY 81

SCHOOLS THAT STOPPED TEACHING TRADES 81
    The Systematic Dismantling 82
THE ACADEMIC–VOCATIONAL CASTE SYSTEM 83
    For Students 83
    For Schools 83
    For Society 83
THE COLLEGE-FOR-ALL MYTH 84
THE ECONOMIC REALITY CHECK 84
    Trade School Advantages 84
    Career Prospects 85
PARENTS WHO MEAN WELL BUT MISS THE MARK 85
    The Information Gap Is Real 86
    The Prestige Trap 86
POLICY THAT PRIORITIZES COLLEGE OVER COMPETENCE 86

- *Current Federal Investment* 87
- *What Policy Change Looks Like* 87
- The Personal Journey 88
- Reality Check: The Digital Generation Isn't Hopeless 89
  - *Modern Recruitment Strategies* 89
- The Technology Integration Opportunity 90
  - *Construction Technology* 90
- Building Comprehensive Solutions 91
  - *At the School Level* 91
  - *At the Family Level* 91
  - *At the Policy Level* 92
- The Rising Tide 92
  - *Recent Trends* 92
  - *Industry Response* 93
- It Takes All of Us 93
  - *Specific Roles* 93
- The Vision of Success 94
- But It's Fixable. If We Choose to Fix It 95

CHAPTER 9: TOOL BELT MEETS TECH—AI, INNOVATION, AND THE FUTURE OF THE TRADES 97

- The Evolution of Tools 97
- The Internet of Things (IoT) on the Jobsite 98
  - *Modern Construction Technology* 98
  - *Advanced Robotics* 99
  - *Smart Tools and IoT* 99
  - *Augmented and Virtual Reality* 99
- The Reality of Automation in Construction 100
  - *Current State of Construction Robotics* 100
  - *What Robots Can Do Now* 100
  - *What They Can't Do* 100
- Maintenance Never Goes Out of Style 101
  - *The Maintenance Reality* 101
- Jobs at Risk vs. Jobs Enhanced 102
  - *Higher Risk Positions* 102
  - *Lower Risk Positions* 102
  - *Enhanced Positions* 103
- Why Human Skills Remain Essential 103
  - *Physical Dexterity and Adaptability* 103
  - *Problem-Solving and Creativity* 103
  - *Human Interaction* 104
  - *Quality Judgment* 104
  - *Contextual Understanding* 104
- Reality Check: Robots Don't Replace Pride 104

THE COLLABORATIVE FUTURE 105
    Examples of Successful Collaboration.. 106
NEW OPPORTUNITIES IN TECH-ENHANCED TRADES.. 106
UPSKILLING FOR THE FUTURE... 107
EMBRACING WHAT'S NEXT—WITHOUT LOSING WHAT MATTERS............................... 108
THE LABOR SHORTAGE SOLUTION.. 109
GLOBAL PERSPECTIVES ON AUTOMATION.. 109
ENVIRONMENTAL AND EFFICIENCY BENEFITS... 110
THE HUMAN ELEMENT THAT CAN'T BE CODED 110
LOOKING FORWARD... 111

CHAPTER 10: REBUILDING RESPECT, ONE TRADE AT A TIME 113
    WHY RESPECT MATTERS: MORE THAN YOU THINK 113
        The Real Cost of Disrespect.. 113
        The Multiplier Effect of Respect... 114
    WORK THAT LEAVES A MARK: THE LEGACY ADVANTAGE 115
        The Tangible Impact Difference... 115
        Modern Legacy Projects 115
    REALITY CHECK: WE LOST A GENERATION TO SCREENS, BUT RECOVERY IS POSSIBLE........ 116
        The Numbers Tell the Story... 116
        But There's Hope in the Data.. 117
        The Gaming Connection 117
    THE ECONOMIC CASE FOR RESPECT 118
        International Examples... 118
        The American Opportunity 118
    BREAKING DOWN THE BARRIERS: SYSTEMIC CHANGES NEEDED................................. 119
        Educational Reform 119
        Media Representation 120
        Workplace Culture 120
    THE DEMOGRAPHIC REVOLUTION: NEW FACES, SAME VALUES 121
        Women in the Trades 121
        Military Veterans... 121
        Second-Career Professionals... 122
        The Common Thread 122
    TECHNOLOGY AS A RESPECT BUILDER 122
        Attracting Digital Natives 123
        Improving Working Conditions 123
        Enhancing Problem-Solving 123
        Creating New Career Paths... 123
    THE ROAD BACK IS BUILT TOGETHER—A COMPREHENSIVE STRATEGY......................... 124
        Individual Actions That Matter.. 124
        Community-Level Changes 125
        Industry-Wide Initiatives... 126
    MEASURING SUCCESS: WHAT VICTORY LOOKS LIKE 127

- *Economic Indicators* *127*
- *Social Indicators* *127*
- *Workplace Indicators* *128*
- *Cultural Indicators* *128*
- THE GENERATIONAL BRIDGE: LEARNING FROM EACH OTHER 128
  - *What Experienced Workers Bring* *128*
  - *What Younger Workers Bring* *129*
  - *Creating Successful Partnerships* *129*
- GLOBAL COMPETITION AND NATIONAL SECURITY 129
  - *The Strategic Reality* *130*
  - *Current Challenges* *130*
  - *The Path Forward* *130*
- BEYOND INDIVIDUAL SUCCESS: BUILDING COMMUNITY 131
  - *What Healthy Trade Communities Look Like* *131*
  - *The Ripple Effects* *132*
- A PERSONAL CHALLENGE: WHAT WILL YOU DO? 132
  - *To Current Tradespeople* *132*
  - *To Parents and Educators* *133*
  - *To Business and Community Leaders* *133*
  - *To Young People* *133*
- THE LONG VIEW: BUILDING FOR GENERATIONS 134
  - *What Success Will Look Like in 20 Years* *134*
  - *The Foundation We're Building* *134*

CONCLUSION: THE CHOICE BEFORE US 137

EPILOGUE: FOR THE ONES WHO SHOWED UP 139

- THE SHIFT IS COMING 139
- THE PROMISE WE MAKE 140
- THE WORK CONTINUES 141

RESOURCES 143

- TRADE UNION RESOURCES 143
- BUILDING TRADES UNIONS 143
  - *International Brotherhood of Boilermakers (IBB)*
  - *https://www.boilermakers.org* *143*
  - *United Brotherhood of Carpenters and Joiners of America (UBC)*
  - *https://www.carpenters.org* *143*
  - *International Brotherhood of Electrical Workers (IBEW)*
  - *https://www.ibew.org* *143*
  - *International Association of Bridge, Structural, Ornamental and Reinforcing Iron Workers https://www.ironworkers.org* *144*
  - *Laborers' International Union of North America (LIUNA)*
  - *https://www.liuna.org* *144*

    United Association of Journeymen and Apprentices of the Plumbing and Pipe Fitting Industry (UA) https://www.ua.org 144
    International Union of Operating Engineers (IUOE) https://www.iuoe.org 144
    Sheet Metal Workers' International Association (SMWIA) https://www.smwia.org 144
    International Union of Painters and Allied Trades (IUPAT) https://www.iupat.org 145
    United Union of Roofers, Waterproofers and Allied Workers https://www.unionroofers.com 145
  ADDITIONAL RESOURCES 145
    Building Trades Unions–North America's Building Trades Unions) https://www.buildingtradeunions.org 145
    Helmets to Hardhats https://www.helmetstohardhats.org 145
    National Center for Construction Education and Research (NCCER) https://www.nccer.org 145
    U.S. Department of Labor–Office of Apprenticeship https://www.apprenticeship.gov 146
    Women Build Nations https://www.womenbuildnations.org 146
    National Association of Women in Construction (NAWIC) https://www.nawic.org 146

ABOUT THE AUTHOR 147

AUTHOR'S NOTE 149

REFERENCES 151

Introduction:
Not a Backup Plan

We've been telling a lie for years: that the trades are a fallback. Plan B: something you do when *college doesn't work out*.

I've heard it whispered at high school graduation parties. I've seen it in the disappointed looks when a bright kid chooses welding over premed. I've felt it in the way people's voices change when they ask what I do for a living—that subtle shift from curiosity to pity, as if I'd somehow settled for less.

But here's the truth I've learned from calloused hands and aching backs, from sunrise job sites and the satisfaction of work well done: *The trades are not second best; they're essential, honorable, and full of potential.* They've built everything we rely on, and they're where a new generation of workers can build strong, secure, and meaningful lives.

If it weren't for the trades, we never would have had the industrial revolution. Neither the Sears Tower—changed in 2009 to the Willis Tower when the naming rights contract with Sears, Roebuck and Company expired (Osmond, 2025)—nor the Empire State Building would have been built. The railroads never would have connected the United States, and the interstate system never would have been constructed. Every bridge you cross, every building you enter, and every wire that brings electricity to your home all exist because someone with skilled hands and practical knowledge made them real.

I am a carpenter's daughter. I've been a carpenter, laborer, and ironworker. I've lived this life, and I've seen what it can offer. But I've also seen how we've systematically devalued it, pushed it to the margins, and convinced entire generations that working with your hands is somehow less worthy than working with spreadsheets.

The Shift Is Coming

A shift is happening, and it's about time.

In May 2025, President Donald Trump made headlines when he announced on Truth Social that he was considering taking $3 billion in federal grant money away from Harvard University and redirecting it to trade schools across the country. His words sparked fierce debate, but the message resonated:

> We've been overfunding prestige and underfunding practicality. I am considering taking Three Billion Dollars of Grant Money away from a very antisemitic Harvard and giving it to TRADE SCHOOLS all across our land. What a great investment that would be for the USA, and so badly needed!!! (Trump, 2025).

Love him or not, that statement struck a chord because it wasn't just about funding; it was about *value*. For too long, we've valued status over substance, credentials over capability, and theory over practice. And now, we're paying the price—with empty job sites, crumbling infrastructure, and an entire generation that doesn't know how things are made, fixed, or built.

The numbers tell the story: According to Tremper (2024) "The share of new hires who are 18-25 year olds has been increasing in high skilled trades. On average, the share of new hires aged 18-25 in the housing construction industry has increased by nearly 4% annually since 2019." Mike Rowe, founder of the mikeroweWORKS Foundation and longtime advocate for skilled trades, captured the urgency perfectly when discussing the need for trade school funding: "If I could reach the panic button, I'd hit it right now" (Bailey, 2024).

Yet misconceptions persist: A 2022 study found that only 42% of people expect skilled trade workers to earn at least $50,000, with 19% believing starting pay is less than $20,000 (*Makers Index*, 2022).

The reality?

Half of skilled trade workers with less than 10 years' experience actually earn at least $50,000 at the start (*Stanley Balck & Decker*, 2022). Meanwhile, construction and manufacturing wages have risen 23.5% and 20.1% respectively above pre-COVID levels (*Construction Wage*, 2024).

I've seen encouraging signs on social media, such as posts about *signing days* for trades apprenticeship programs, just like the signing days colleges have—young people celebrating their acceptance into electrical programs with the same pride others show for Ivy League admissions, and parents beaming as their kids choose concrete over calculus. It's happening, slowly but surely.

My godson, 17, is working with electricians during the summer between his sophomore and junior year of high school as a pre-apprentice, learning the trade and seeing if it is a fit for him. Along with that, it gives him a leg up and almost a guaranteed place if he decides to formally join the electrician apprenticeship when he graduates.

In addition, my grandson, 12, says he wants to work in construction someday. That's encouraging.

More Than Work: A Way of Life

The trades offer more than work; they offer *purpose*. They offer a chance to build something lasting—not just physically, but personally. They offer young adults a path to self-sufficiency, the ability to buy a house or a new car sooner rather than later. Therefore, the trades build self-esteem, confidence, and accountability. Above all, they build respect—for the work, for the craft, and for oneself.

As Mike Rowe puts it, "The idea that a four-year degree is the only path to worthwhile knowledge is insane" (Rowe, 2023). He's right. The Bureau of Labor Statistics reports that the median annual wage for construction and extraction occupations was $55,680 in 2023, higher than the median for all occupations at $48,060 (*Occupational Outlook*,

2024). More importantly, these are careers with remarkable job security: "You're not going to AI-out a plumber," as Rowe notes, giving skilled workers an advantage that white-collar workers increasingly lack (Bailey, 2024).

When you can look at a building and point to the steel you helped raise, the foundation you helped pour, and the electrical system you helped install, that's not just a job; that's a legacy. That's the kind of work that connects you to something bigger than yourself, something that will outlast you.

Breaking the Cycle

But we have work to do. We need to break the cycle of shame and misunderstanding that has pushed the trades to the sidelines. We need to tell a different story, one that honors the intelligence, skill, and dedication it takes to master a trade. One that recognizes the economic opportunity, job security, and personal fulfillment that skilled work provides.

This book is for every young person who has ever felt out of place in a classroom but came alive in a workshop. For every parent who's been told their child is "too smart" for the trades, as if intelligence and craftsmanship are mutually exclusive. For every worker who has poured concrete, pulled wire, raised steel, or shaped the bones of this country and never gotten the recognition they deserved.

If you're reading this, you already feel the pull of honest work. Maybe you've lived it. Maybe you're ready to rediscover it. Maybe you're tired of the lies and ready for the truth.

The Foundation We Stand On

Let this book be the start of a new narrative. One that lifts those who work with their hands. One that tells the truth about what it takes to build a life—literally and figuratively. One that proves, once and for all, that the trades were never a backup plan.

They were the foundation all along.

And it's time we started building on it.

Chapter 1:
Built, Not a Backup Plan

Somewhere along the way, we started treating the trades like a consolation prize.

College became the gold standard. Anything else? Second best. The road you take if you weren't *college material*, be it military service or the trades.

That narrative is not just wrong; it's dangerous. And it's costing us more than we realize.

I watch it play out every day. High school guidance counselors who steer bright kids away from apprenticeships toward four-year degrees they can't afford. Parents who apologize when their child chooses welding over prelaw. A culture that has somehow convinced itself that the people who literally build our world are settling for less.

The First Choice That No One Talks About

For decades, young people have been coached to believe that the only respectable future lies behind a desk. Meanwhile, the careers that keep the lights on, the water running, and the buildings standing have quietly faded into the background of career day presentations and college prep seminars.

But the truth is this: Skilled trades are not what you settle for; they are what you *build on*. For every young person who has learned about the trades from their parents, it's insulting to think that their only option is college. Most young people who grow up learning about the trades at home find deep satisfaction in the work and confidence and responsibility it instills.

I learned construction skills from my dad. He would take me to his job sites as a small child. He would bring the excess materials home, and my brother and I would build using them. We constructed a fort for us and our friends when we were nine and eight, respectively. It was incredible! That early exposure didn't limit our options; it expanded them. It gave us confidence, problem-solving skills, and the knowledge that we could create something with our own hands.

The trades are paths that lead to ownership. To leadership. To mastery. They offer freedom, stability, and pride. And unlike many white-collar jobs, they still carry a visible, tangible legacy. You can point to what you made and say, "That's mine."

I still do that today when I look at particular highway bridges that I had a hand in building, and I am proud of that. They were built 20 years ago, and they're still carrying traffic, still serving their purpose. That's not just work; that's legacy.

Debt-Free and in Demand

While many four-year graduates are walking across a stage and into decades of debt, young tradespeople are walking onto jobsites—and earning a living. Unlike college, which can cost thousands of dollars, apprenticeships are a debt-free, industry-driven training option that allows workers to earn while they learn.

The U.S. Bureau of Labor Statistics projects over 500,000 new skilled trade openings annually through 2032 (*Torpey*, 2024). These aren't fallback roles but careers with a critical need.

The numbers tell a compelling story. The Union building trades' *earn while you learn* registered apprenticeship model offers competitive wages and benefits without the burden of college debt. Compare that reality to the average college graduate who leaves school with over $37,000, or more, in student loan debt and no guarantee of employment (*Federal Student Loan portfolio*, n.d.).

Some apprenticeships pay as you learn, offer benefits from day one, and end with zero student loan balance. Apprentices usually train under the direction of experienced workers, earning about half of what a fully qualified worker does, and apprentices earn pay increases as they advance in their training. That means you're making money while gaining skills, not paying for the privilege of sitting in a lecture hall.

Reality Check: Value Isn't Always Found in a Degree

A whole generation has been sold the idea that the only way forward is a degree. But that's only true if we define success by a single, narrow track. We've got engineers who can't change a car tire. Designers who've never touched a tool. MBA graduates who've never managed anything more complex than their class schedule. And young people who feel lost because they don't fit in a classroom, but haven't been shown another way, working minimum wage jobs when they can do so much more if just shown the way.

We need to be honest: Working with your hands is not a downgrade; it's a *different kind* of intelligence, and it's every bit as vital. Some of the best engineers I have known and worked with on construction sites could design, fabricate, and build—without a four-year degree in engineering—and it worked, the first time, every time. That's experience, that's critical thinking, and that's problem-solving in real-time under pressure.

These are the people who understand physics not from a textbook but from watching a crane lift steel into place. Those who grasp engineering principles not from theory but from making sure a structure stays standing. Those who know materials science from working with concrete, steel, and wood in every weather condition imaginable.

The Skills Gap Reality

Here's what the *college for everyone* crowd doesn't want to admit: We're facing a massive skills shortage in the trades. These dynamics are exacerbated by the significant number of retirements and steep turnover rates—often much higher than the national separation rate of 3.3% (*Job openings and labor turnover - February 2020*, 2025).

Baby boomers are retiring in droves, taking with them decades of hands-on knowledge, and we're not replacing them fast enough (*The Home Builders Institute*, 2024).

This isn't just a workforce problem; it's an infrastructure crisis waiting to happen. When your power goes out, your pipes burst, or your roof needs repair, you don't call someone with a liberal arts degree. You call someone who knows their craft, shows up prepared, and gets the job done right the first time. Rain or shine. Heat or snow. Because that's what the job—and the world—requires.

Built by Choice, Not Default

I didn't fall into the trades; I *chose* them. And I would choose them again.

Because when the waterline's broken or the framework needs tying, the world doesn't call a marketing major; it calls a *tradesperson*.

After college, when I couldn't find a job I enjoyed in my chosen field, I defaulted back to what I knew: working outside with my dad and my brother. I was remodeling houses, building garages, roofing, roughing in, pouring concrete, and doing finish work. It was heaven! The satisfaction of seeing something take shape under your hands, of solving problems that textbooks never covered, of building something that would last—that's when I knew I was home.

I went on to become an ironworker—a profession I chose deliberately. I did that for 10 years. It took me all over the United States and even to Antarctica. I worked on projects that challenged every skill I had, alongside people who taught me things no classroom ever could. I earned respect not because of a diploma on my wall but because I could do the work, do it well, and do it safely.

The Intelligence of the Hands

A particular kind of intelligence, instinct, comes from working with your hands, and our society has forgotten how to value it. It's that intelligence that can look at a blueprint and see not just lines on paper, but the sequence of operations needed to make it real. The intelligence that can diagnose a problem by sound, feel, and experience that can't be downloaded or googled.

This is the intelligence that built the Hoover Dam, the Golden Gate Bridge, and the skyscrapers that define our cities. It's that intelligence that keeps our infrastructure running, our homes comfortable, and our workplaces functional. And it's that intelligence that will be needed to rebuild America's aging infrastructure, to construct the clean energy systems of the future, and to maintain and improve the current environment we all depend on.

More Than a Job—a Way of Being

The trades don't just offer work; they offer a way of life, of being in a world that's increasingly rare. They offer the satisfaction of completion, the pride of craftsmanship, and the security of skills that can't be outsourced or automated away. They offer a connection to the physical world that screen-based work simply cannot provide.

When you've spent your day installing electrical systems, you understand how buildings work in ways that most people never will. When you've poured concrete, you appreciate the engineering that goes into foundations. When you've welded steel, you understand the strength and precision required to join materials that will bear loads for decades.

This isn't just about making a living; it's about making a life that has weight, substance, and meaning.

> *There's honor in showing up and building something real. We don't need more backup plans; we need more builders.*

Chapter 2:

The Lost Respect for the Trades

There was a time when knowing how to use your hands meant something. When being a welder, carpenter, or operator didn't just earn you a paycheck; it earned you *respect*. You were part of the backbone, the infrastructure, and the crew that built the country from the ground up.

Somewhere along the line, that changed.

We started telling our kids that a four-year degree was the only ticket to success. Shop classes disappeared from high schools. *Dirty jobs* became something to avoid, not admire, and little by little, the narrative shifted from *builders of America* to *fallback careers*.

I felt that shift firsthand. Not just in how people outside the trades looked at us, but in how young people stopped showing up to learn. Somewhere between status and student debt, we lost the plot.

Parents always want better for their children. Sometimes, that *better* means following in your father's or mother's footsteps, even with the long hours, the missed games or birthdays, and even missed holidays, because a turnaround or shutdown doesn't care about work-life balance. The money is good, and winter is coming: You need to work while you can; there may be a layoff soon. It's part of a *tradesperson's* life. But it's also a life of pride and skill: It's being proud of providing a good life for your family, and a genuine contribution to society.

A Culture That Forgot Its Builders

Not long ago, it wasn't uncommon for high schools to offer woodshop, auto tech, metalworking, or basic electrical wiring. These programs provided real-world skills—and real-world career options.

Now, most of those classrooms are storage closets, their equipment auctioned off or left to rust.

The statistics tell a stark story. Between 1990 and 2009, as the average number of academic credits earned by high-school students increased, the number of vocational credits declined, coinciding with a 32% drop in federal funding for industrial arts programs since 1985 (Gray & Herr, 2006).

In Seattle, for example, only 4 of the 17 shop classes that once existed are left. Younger generations are largely unaware of what shop class is, why it exists, and how it has evolved over the years (Coshow, 2019).

In the 2024–2025 academic year, approximately 19.1 million students were enrolled in U.S. post-secondary institutions, including nearly 16 million undergraduates (*College Enrollment Rates*, 2024). In contrast, registered apprenticeship programs had about 593,000 active participants in FY 2021 (*Apprenticeship Continues*, 2021).

That's not a coincidence but a reflection of a cultural push-away from blue-collar work. Even when parents and teachers recognize the value of trades work, many hesitate to encourage the students, thinking it's settling for less.

Yet the truth is: We haven't just devalued the work; we've discouraged entire generations from seeing themselves in it. According to Holmes (2019). "There is a huge shortage in skilled trades because the next generation is being pushed exclusively into careers that require a university education, even though the skilled trades are filled with brilliant, hardworking, successful men and women."

The Pervasive Stigma

The cultural shift didn't happen overnight; it was systematic and deliberate. There is a perception that trade jobs are dirty and dangerous, or that they require little skill or thinking and offer virtually no career advancement (Rosenbaum, 2001).

This thinking is so wrong on many levels. Yes, trade jobs can be dirty and dangerous. However, by learning the trade and how to do the work safely and with deliberate action, trade work is quite safe and prosperous as it presents a clear path for career advancement—from apprentice to journeyman/woman, to lead, foreman, general foreman, superintendent, and eventually to roles in the office or as a union leader. Additionally, pay increases often accompany these advancements.

Pop culture depicts workers as bumbling, poor, stupid, lazy, sleazy, and rude. This media portrayal has created a toxic feedback loop where skilled work is consistently undervalued and misunderstood, which is an insult to any of us out there that has worked in the trades.

The reality couldn't be more different: While 89% of workers say they work with advanced technology (*Makers Index*, 2022), most young people have outdated perceptions of the trades. These aren't the jobs of the 1950s; today's trades require sophisticated technical knowledge, continuous learning, and problem-solving skills that rival any profession.

Furthermore, the income misconceptions are particularly damaging. "Young people underestimate the income potential for a skilled trade career; however, half of the current skilled trade workers with less than 10 years' experience have earned at least $50,000 to start (*Ramond and Dreher*, 2022)." Meanwhile, college graduates have been drowning in debt with no guarantee of employment in their field.

Reality Check: A Generation Raised on Screens

We didn't just lose shop class; we lost *hands-on interest*. A whole generation was raised on video games, instant gratification, and digital distractions. The call to work with your hands, to solve real-world problems, to sweat and build—that voice got drowned out by screen time.

This isn't about blaming technology; it's about balance. It's about reconnecting young people with the physical world and the deep human reward of *making something that lasts*. When everything in your life can be deleted, updated, or replaced with a click, there's something profoundly grounding about creating something permanent with your own hands.

I grew up in a time when kids still knew where their food came from. When fixing something was the first option, not the last. When understanding how things worked wasn't just curiosity but a necessity. Now, I meet young adults who've never held a wrench, never seen a construction site up close, and never experienced the satisfaction of building something from scratch.

We've created a generation that consumes but doesn't create, that uses but doesn't understand, that depends on but doesn't respect the infrastructure that makes its digital life possible. Every app it uses, every video it streams, and every social media post it shares depends on physical infrastructure built and maintained by skilled tradespeople.

The Prestige Trap

Somewhere along the way, *success* has become synonymous with business suits and bachelor's degrees. There's nothing wrong with pursuing a traditional academic path, but there *is* something wrong with pretending it's the only path that matters.

I've known college grads with 6 figures in debt and no job. I've also known apprentices in their early '20s clearing $80,000 a year debt-free—and doing work they love. Yet too often, the suit gets the applause. The *tradesperson* gets the shrug.

Trades work is not *dirty* work; it's building the fabric of our nation. It's hard work, it's rewarding work, and it's relevant work. However, our culture has somehow convinced itself that work requiring physical skill is somehow less worthy than work requiring only mental effort.

What most people do not understand is that there is *a lot* of mental effort involved in the trades. Critical thinking skills are called upon every time a beam doesn't fit in the space it is *supposed* to go, or the dimensions are wrong for a concrete pour.

That's the trap. We equated *prestige* with *value* and forgot that what's valuable is often what's taken for granted: clean water, power, housing, safety, and infrastructure. None of that comes from behind a desk. All of it comes from skilled hands.

I went to school with kids who thought meat and milk came from the grocery store, with no concept of the farmers who produced and processed the food and milk they consumed every day. That disconnect—between what we consume and who provides it—is at the heart of our cultural problem with the trades.

The Dangerous Consequences

This cultural shift has created real problems that extend far beyond hurt feelings or wounded pride. The death of vocational education is directly linked to the struggles of the American middle class (Crawford, 2009). When we stopped training young people for skilled trades, we eliminated one of the most reliable paths to middle-class prosperity.

The infrastructure consequences are becoming impossible to ignore. Our roads, bridges, electrical grids, and water systems are aging rapidly. Moreover, the people who built them are retiring, and we're not training replacements fast enough. The number of students pursuing 2-year vocational degrees in precision production has fallen 18% even as demand for these skills continues to grow (College Board Advocacy and Access Communities, 2023).

In summary, we're facing a perfect storm: aging infrastructure, retiring workers, and a culture that has spent decades discouraging young people from pursuing the very careers we desperately need (American Society of Civil Engineers, 2021).

The result? Critical shortages in every trade, from electricians to plumbers to welders to heavy equipment operators.

The Respect Deficit

The lack of respect for trades work isn't just about social status; it's about a fundamental misunderstanding of what these jobs require.

Modern trades demand:

- **Continuous learning:** Technology changes rapidly, and tradespeople must constantly update their skills.

- **Problem-solving:** Every job site presents unique challenges that require creative solutions.

- **Physical and mental toughness:** Working in all weather conditions while maintaining precision and safety.

- **Leadership:** Experienced tradespeople often manage teams, coordinate with other trades, and make critical decisions.

- **Business acumen:** Many tradespeople become contractors, managing their own businesses and building successful enterprises.

Yet our culture continues to perpetuate the myth that these are jobs for people who *can't do anything else.*

The reality is that good tradespeople could succeed in almost any field—they choose the trades because they find meaning in building, creating, and solving real-world problems.

Reclaiming Respect

This isn't about nostalgia; it's about necessity. We need skilled tradesmen and women to carry the torch of building and maintaining our national infrastructure. We live in an aging society. Not just the people, but the roads, buildings, and bridges need constant maintenance. Our grids are stretched. Our housing is short. And we are running out of the very people who know how to fix it all (*The Home Builders Institute*, 2024).

We need to flip the narrative, which means:

- **Talking about the trades as vital, not optional:** Every conversation about infrastructure, housing, and economic development should acknowledge the skilled workers who make it possible.

- **Highlighting career success stories that don't include college:** We need to celebrate the electrician who started his own company, the welder who became a project manager, and the carpenter who built a construction empire.

- **Teaching kids that a stable, respected, and rewarding life is possible in the trades:** This starts in elementary school, with career days that include real tradespeople sharing their stories.

- **Backing up those stories with resources, funding, and mentorship:** We need to invest in vocational education, apprenticeship programs, and pathways from high school to skilled careers.

Respect will come when we stop treating the trades as backup plans and start recognizing them as first choices. When we stop apologizing for working with our hands and start celebrating the intelligence, skill, and dedication it requires.

The Path Forward

Changing cultural attitudes takes time, but it starts with individuals: every parent who encourages their child to consider the trades, every teacher who talks about apprenticeships alongside college, and every guidance counselor who doesn't automatically steer bright students away from vocational paths.

It starts with us, the people who have lived this life, who know its rewards and challenges and understand its value. We must tell our stories louder, more proudly, and more persistently. We must push back against the narrative that working with your hands is somehow less than working with your mind.

Because the truth is, the best tradespeople do both: They think *and* build. They solve problems *and* create solutions. They use their minds *and* their hands in perfect harmony to make the world work.

This country wasn't typed into existence; it was built—welded, framed, poured, and wired. And if we want to keep building it, we'd better start honoring the hands that still know how.

Chapter 3:

Women Who Weld—Sisterhood in Steel

It's not just a *man's* world.

For a long time, women in the trades were treated like ghosts: there, but rarely seen, rarely counted, and rarely welcomed. They showed up, laced their boots, hoisted their tools, and did the job like anyone else—but with more eyes watching, more doubts to silence, and more to prove just to be seen as equals.

I was one of them. One of only a few women in my Ironworker union actively working at the time. It was great. It was tough. And it was worth every minute. Every new job I went to, I had to go in with an attitude. My business agent sent a journeyman ironworker to do a job; it just happened to be me: a *journeywoman*. I had to earn my place on every job I went to; usually, it only took a day or two, and then it would be okay. The guys would accept me as one of them, part of the team, and they would defend me just like they would anyone else on the team. Sometimes, but not very often, they wouldn't accept me; however, they would tolerate my presence.

Not Just a Man's World

There's a stubborn idea that construction is for men—that steel, concrete, and grit belong to one gender. But step onto a jobsite today, and you'll find women welding, driving, rigging, running wire, fabricating, and leading.

Still, the numbers tell a story of both progress and persistent challenges. In 2024, women represented 11.2% of the construction workforce—the highest level ever recorded. That's 1.343 million women, an increase of 56,000 from the previous year (NAWIC, 2024).

Over the past decade, the number of women in construction has increased by 45%, growing from 929,000 in 2015 to over 1.3 million today (*Annual Report 2024*, 2024).

But dig deeper, and the picture becomes more complex. While women make up 68% of sales and office positions in construction, they represent only 3.9% of those who work with tools on construction sites (*Women in Construction*, 2014). That gap isn't the result of a lack of interest but a lack of invitation—and sometimes, a lack of welcome.

Too often, women are steered away from physical work. Or worse, told they're "not strong enough," "not tough enough," or "not built for it." Women are stronger than you know, mostly out of sheer determination and a will to survive.

But here's the truth: What we lack in numbers, we make up for in drive, detail, and resilience. We don't just show up; we stay. We don't just prove ourselves; we teach others to believe they belong, too. Some of the best welders I know are women. I have heard the same sentiment expressed by men as well. Women are meticulous, steady, and they don't rush. And sometimes, we are the only ones who can fit in a small space!

The Data Behind the Drive

Women now hold 29% of C-suite positions in construction companies, compared with 17% in 2015 (Van Durme et al., 2023). Progress has been slower at entry and managerial levels, but momentum is building.

The geographical patterns tell an interesting story. Alaska and Hawaii show the largest percentage of women in construction, at 14.9% and 13.1% respectively *(2024's Percentage of Women in Construction: The Rising Stats,* 2024). The Pacific Northwest also shows higher participation rates than other regions. In Florida, 3 metropolitan areas lead the nation: Jacksonville at 16.9%, Orlando at 15%, and North Port at 14.3% *(2024's Percentage of Women in Construction: The Rising Stats*, 2024).

Urban areas consistently show higher participation rates, often linked to greater access to education, training programs, and diverse professional networks. This suggests that opportunity and environment play crucial roles in women's entry into the trades (*Women in Construction*, 2023).

The Hard and the Honest

Let's be honest, it's not always easy.

The gear isn't made for us. The bathrooms might not exist. You hear things you shouldn't have to. According to a 2023 report from the Institute for Women's Policy Research, 26.5% of *tradeswomen* reported significant levels of workplace harassment or discrimination (*Women in Construction*, 2023). You carry an extra load just walking on site, but if you have a good crew, they will still respect you and defend you when you bring out the *mom* voice and tell them, "That's enough."

Environmental conditions remain challenging. Job site culture, discrimination, harassment, and limited access to supportive services such as childcare continue to serve as barriers to entry and retention. Women tend to be more heavily represented in administrative and project management roles precisely because the environment on construction sites, including the lack of accessible female-focused hygiene options and the male-dominant culture, remains an obstacle for women seeking hands-on positions (*Annual Report 2024*, 2024).

Nevertheless, you also find something few people ever do: a deep pride in doing real, hard, honest work—and doing it well. You earn your space. You earn your name. And you never forget the women who helped you get there, even if they were few.

The hard-earned respect of your fellow brothers in the trade can be everything. They don't show it, but they will have your back. I have experienced that.

In 2005, I was on a parking garage project in Florida; I was the only woman on the whole job site. I walked by a different contractor crew taking a break, and they started talking and making comments. Because I couldn't understand what they were saying, they thought they got away with something. A manager from another company heard them; he followed me back up to my work area and told my foreman what was going on. Subsequently, my foreman and several of my crewmates went down to the offending crew and took them to task—they stood up for me. I barely knew these guys; I was a visitor to their local union, and they stood up for me. It was humbling and greatly appreciated at the same time. I have never forgotten them for that.

Breaking Down Barriers Through Technology and Innovation

One encouraging trend is the growing recognition that many barriers women face are not insurmountable; they're structural problems with structural solutions. Construction companies are beginning to invest in proper facilities, appropriate safety equipment designed for women's bodies, and policies that support work-life balance. In this context, the new Occupational Safety and Health Administration's ruling on proper fitting of personal protective equipment for everyone, not just for women, is a huge win for women in the construction trades (*Personal Protective Equipment*, 2023).

The rise of technology in construction is also creating new opportunities. Process automation, vendor management, and tech integration roles are leveraging collaboration and coordination skills—areas where women have traditionally excelled. As one industry expert noted, "There are huge opportunities, especially in technology and process automation. The construction industry is notoriously slow to adopt new systems, so anyone willing to take the time to understand workflows and apply automation can make a massive impact" (Martincevic & Madrigal, 2025).

Furthermore, the pandemic accelerated this trend, as massive labor shifts led many people to reconsider traditional career paths. Many women reentering the workforce are now more open to industries they hadn't previously considered, including construction.

Sisterhood in Steel

There's a quiet bond among women in the trades. A nod across the site. A helping hand on a beam. A knowing look when someone underestimates you, and you rise anyway.

Let's hear about my friend Jeanne's experience:

> Jeanne Park, Ironworker, San Francisco, CA:
>
> I joined Ironworkers Local 377 in San Francisco in December 1995.
>
> Cranes littered the city, and projects were coming up everywhere. Affirmative Action had not been struck down yet by Prop 209, so contractors were still half-heartedly looking for women and minorities to fulfill quotas. I believe that was the main reason the structural company on the City Hall retrofit agreed to sponsor me into the trade.
>
> I was fascinated by working with metal and had taken welding classes at a JVC [Joint Vocational College] in Ohio. I knew the basics of how things came together, and I was as green as they come when it came to working on a construction site.
>
> There were no YouTube videos to consult. Social media hadn't become widely available. My resources for learning were the poorly constructed textbooks of the apprenticeship and men who were, at best, reluctant to teach me the trade and how to thrive "for my own good."
>
> There were three other women in my classes at the time. One woman hated me and called me "a suck-up goody two-shoes"

because I studied the books as best I could and asked questions and talked to my instructors. The second woman did well getting along with everyone and ran work but burned out having to constantly battle for her position and her existence in the trade. The last woman, her family ran a large steel company, and many had high hopes for her, but she died of an overdose on an out-of-town job.

There were a couple of older women in the local who had been there at least a decade longer than I. The attitude they had was that it was a man's trade and I needed to be more like the men—more violent, more callous. They had very little encouragement for me. [I was told to] "Suck it up," if I wanted to hang with the big men.

I joined up with tradeswomen organizations and sought solidarity with women in other trades. I was told to my face that there was no such thing as women ironworkers because the trade is too tough and the guys are all assholes.

Thank goodness, I loved the work itself. The solid feel of moving structures into place. The satisfaction of a weld gleaming in place. One apprenticeship instructor, Henry Ellis, became my mentor—he was a Korean War vet and was very curious as to why I would choose the work I did.

I tried starting a women's committee in my local with Henry's encouragement, so that we could build on each other's knowledge and support each other when things got rough. It was very difficult to get women together since many of us lived at the limits of the local area, or were working overtime, or were single parents. One of the older women explained to me that I should just stop complaining about unfairness and injustice because nothing would ever change, and men would never respect our existence in the trade.

Jeanne Park

In the end, things did change; the *guys* in the Ironworkers did respect us. I was an Ironworker. I got into the trade in 1997. When I took my withdrawal in 2008, it was there... the respect.

Organizations like *The National Association of Women in Construction (NAWIC) and Tradeswomen Build Nations* are working to amplify that bond. *NAWIC*, founded in 1953 by 16 women in Fort Worth, Texas, now has more than 6,000 members across 120+ chapters nationwide (*Annual Report 2024*, 2024). They offer mentoring, education, visibility, career growth, industry resources, advocacy, and connectivity. Therefore, they say what many of us have always felt: "You are not alone."

Note that *NAWIC* extends beyond the United States, with affiliate associations in the United Kingdom, Australia, New Zealand, South Africa, and Canada. Their core purpose is to strengthen and amplify the success of women in the construction industry through immediate access to an invaluable network of women in various stages of their careers (*Annual Report 2024*, 2024).

The *National Taskforce on Tradeswomen's Issues* is another important coalition promoting public policies and best practices toward equity in apprenticeship, training, workforce development, and workplace experience (National Taskforce on Tradeswomen's Issues, n.d.).

These organizations understand that having clear data creates accountability and helps ensure that women have access to sustainable careers with adequate working hours, workplace policies that support work-family balance, and freedom from bias and harassment.

Local chapters offer networking and mentorship opportunities from women who understand the local culture and environment. As Mercedes Gamor, NAWIC Puget Sound Chapter President, puts it: "There is power in connection" (*Annual Report 2024*, 2024). These connections provide professional development opportunities, community-building events, and volunteer opportunities that strengthen both individual careers and the broader community of women in construction.

Rising Through the Ranks

Data shows that when given the opportunity and support, women thrive in construction. In 2021, the number of women working in trades occupations reached the highest level ever, at just over 314,000 (National Taskforce on Tradeswomen's Issues, 2022). In the 5 years leading up to 2014, the number of *tradeswomen* increased by almost 1/3—32.1%. More women now work as *tradeswomen* than as dental hygienists or veterinarians (*Women in Construction*, 2014).

This matters because construction trades careers do not require a college degree, are accessible through earn-as-you-learn apprenticeships, and, especially in union jobs, provide good pay with benefits. Hence, access to family-sustaining blue-collar careers is critical for women's economic security.

Organizations like *Power Up*, founded by Dr. Mittie Cannon in 2015, are making a difference at the grassroots level. *Power Up* introduces young girls and their mothers to the construction trades, spanning 5 states in addition to Guam. Over 1,000 girls in preschool through 12th grade have been introduced to construction through these programs (*Program Impact Report*, 2024).

As Dr. Cannon explains, "I wanted to let other women know that there's this opportunity out there where you can make high wages, meet other people, do interesting work, and travel" (*2024's Percentage*, 2024).

Mentorship Matters

Mentorship matters. Visibility matters. And sisterhood? It's not just support; it's survival. We pass down lessons, lift each other up, and hold the door open wider than it was for us.

The women who came before us faced even greater obstacles. They worked without networks, organizations, and often without basic amenities. They proved that women could do the work, handle the physical demands, and earn respect on the hardest job sites. We stand on their shoulders.

Women in World War II

Furthermore, when the world went to war, women went to work.

During World War II, with millions of men deployed overseas, it was women who stepped into the factories, shipyards, and welding shops. They built tanks, repaired engines, riveted planes, ran cranes, and held the line—not just for production, but for an entire nation's survival.

More than 6 million women entered the workforce, many of them in skilled trades (Santana, 2016). They proved they could do the work—not temporarily, but excellently—and they didn't just keep America running; they rebuilt what it meant to be a worker.

In this setting, *Rosie the Riveter* became a symbol, but the truth ran deeper. These women weren't just icons; they were ironworkers, machinists, welders, electricians, and mechanics. However, when the war ended, many were told to step aside.

But the legacy hasn't gone away.

Every woman in the trades today walks in those footsteps—with grit, pride, and the same quiet determination that helped win a war.

Now, it's our turn to be the women we needed when we were starting out. To be the mentors who explain not just how to read blueprints but how to navigate the unwritten rules. To be the advocates who push for better policies, better facilities, and better opportunities. To be the examples that show the next generation what's possible.

Reality Check: If She Can't See It, She Can't Be It

We've lost too many skilled, capable women because no one told them they belonged.

The statistics on representation matter because representation creates possibility. When young girls see women welding, operating heavy equipment, and managing construction projects, something fundamental shifts in their understanding of what they can become.

Thus, we need posters, programs, and policies that show young girls the whole picture: Operating equipment, steelwork, pipe fitting, rigging, electrical work, and welding aren't just for the boys. They're for the bold. For the skilled. For anyone ready to step up.

In this context, educational initiatives are making a difference. Local and state programs focused on getting women into the trades are rising nationwide. No longer are the jobs just in administrative roles; these programs specifically target hands-on trade positions.

The industry is responding to labor shortages by actively seeking women, driven by diversity initiatives and growing awareness of the benefits of a more inclusive workforce. Companies are recognizing that they need all available talent to meet construction demands.

The Economic Imperative

The economic case for women in construction is compelling. The Bureau of Labor Statistics projects a 4% growth in the construction industry from 2021 to 2031, translating to approximately 168,500 new jobs each year (BigRentz, 2024). Given this rapid and consistent growth, companies are more inclined than ever to actively seek and recruit women.

On the other hand, the gender wage gap in construction is narrowing, with a 16.8% reduction in just one year, according to recent data (*Women in Construction*, 2023). While challenges remain, the financial opportunities are real and growing. Women in construction often earn more than their counterparts in traditionally female-dominated fields, with the added benefit of job security in an essential industry.

That's the beauty of the trades: It doesn't matter who the *journeyperson* is—man or woman—they earn the same wage.

The Path Forward

Change is happening, but it requires sustained effort. Therefore, we need continued investment in programs that introduce girls to construction careers early, like *Power Up*, mentioned earlier in the Chapter. We need companies that don't just hire women but create environments where they can thrive. We need policies that support work-life balance for everyone and address the unique challenges women face in construction.

Most importantly, we need women who are willing to be visible, tell their stories, and mentor the next generation. Every woman who succeeds in the trades makes it easier for the women who follow.

The construction industry benefits greatly from access to the skilled work of women. Studies consistently show that diverse teams outperform homogeneous ones (Horwitz & Horwitz, 2007). Moreover, as the industry faces ongoing labor shortages, the untapped potential of women represents both an opportunity and a necessity.

Our Legacy

We are not just workers; we are pioneers. Every beam we set, every weld we lay down, and every project we complete is proof that construction is not just a man's world. It's a world built by skilled hands, regardless of gender.

Moreover, representation is more than a statistic; it's a signal. And every time a girl sees a woman in the trades, something clicks: *"Maybe I can do that, too."*

We are forging strong women; we are showing our sons and daughters that women are strong, independent, and worth listening to and learning from.

And that's how we change everything. One girl, one woman, one opportunity at a time.

We don't just belong in the trades; we make them stronger.

Chapter 4:
From Hard Sell to Hard Hat—Rethinking Recruitment

Ask a classroom of high schoolers what they want to be, and you'll hear: doctor, lawyer, YouTube influencer, maybe engineer. What you likely won't hear is: welder, lineman, heavy equipment operator.

It's not that these jobs aren't valuable—they are. It's not that they don't pay well—they do. It's that they're invisible in the cultural conversation about success, and that's a failure of recruitment, representation, and education.

The irony? While we've been pushing college for everyone, a quiet revolution has been building. Generation Z is starting to wake up to what we've known all along—that the trades offer something that many four-year degrees can't: immediate relevance, financial stability, and work that matters.

When Did We Stop Showing the Trades?

Decades ago, shop class was a staple in public schools. Auto tech, woodshop, and metalworking weren't electives; they were pathways. But today, fewer than one in five students have access to vocational education in high school (*The State of Career Technical Education*, 2020), and fewer still are introduced to trades as a *first* option.

The numbers tell a stark story. Between 1982 and 1992, while total high school credits increased by 11% and academic credits rose by 22%, vocational credits declined by almost 17% (National Center for Education Statistics, 1994). By 1992, vocational coursework made up only 16% of total coursework completed by high school graduates, down from 21% in 1982 (National Center for Education Statistics, 1994). In addition, since 1985, federal funding for vocational programs has dropped by 32% (Kreisman & Stange, 2019).

Instead, we have sold a single story: college. A four-year degree. White-collar dreams. And anything else? That's for people who *can't cut it*.

That message has done real damage. We've stigmatized skilled work. We've erased pathways to middle-class stability. And in doing so, we've failed to meet the growing demand for workers in infrastructure, utilities, manufacturing, and construction.

The academic–vocational caste system, as education experts call it, has become one of the most corrosive problems in education (Rosenbaum, 2001).

We've created a hierarchy where working with your hands is somehow seen as less valuable than working with spreadsheets, even though our communities and economies depend on an enormous diversity of talents, roles, and occupations.

The Tide Is Turning

But something interesting is happening. While traditional higher education faces declining enrollment, public two-year colleges saw a 7.8% drop, and public four-year institutions declined by 3.4%—many trade programs are experiencing growth (*Term Enrollment Estimates: Spring 2023*, 2023). In this context, the number of students enrolled in vocational-focused community colleges increased by 16% from 2022 to 2023 (Johnston, 2024).

Additionally, specific trade programs are witnessing even more dramatic increases (*Term Enrollment Estimates: Spring 2023*, 2023):

- Construction trades enrollment increased by 19.3%.

- Mechanic and repair programs grew by 11.5%.

- Culinary programs expanded by 12.7%.

This isn't just a statistical blip; it's a generational shift. Meet the "tool belt generation," as some are calling them. These are young people who've looked at crushing college debt and uncertain job prospects and said, "There has to be a better way."

In a December 2020 survey, 57% of college students said higher education was no longer *worth the cost* (Fishman et al., 2021). Meanwhile, more than half of Gen Z believe it's possible to get a well-paying job with only a high school diploma, provided one acquires other skills (Johnston, 2024).

The Digital Natives Discover the Trades

Here's what's fascinating about Generation Z: They're digital natives who grew up with instant access to information, yet they're increasingly drawn to hands-on work. They've seen artificial intelligence threaten white-collar jobs and witnessed friends graduating from college with massive debt and limited opportunities. To them, manual labor isn't a step backward; it's job security.

They've also seen through the college marketing machine in ways previous generations haven't. This is a generation that values authenticity over everything else. Hence, only 42% of Gen Z individuals say they trust brands and businesses (Izon, n.d.), making them far more skeptical than previous generations. They want transparency, real results, and proof that an investment will pay off.

The trades offer all of that. While college graduates face an uncertain job market, skilled tradespeople are in high demand, with clear career paths and immediate earning potential. Wind turbine installers, for example, can make more than $100,000 a year, and the job market is exploding with demand (*Occupational Outlook Handbook*, 2024).

Marketing That Misses the Mark

When was the last time you saw a commercial that made the trades look exciting or a guidance counselor passionately promote an apprenticeship program? I don't ever remember a time when the trades were actively promoted to the masses. It was always word of mouth; you knew someone who could help you get in to talk to someone. And sometimes, all it took was nepotism—your dad, uncle, grandfather, or maybe your mother or sister was in the trade, and you were a shoo-in. No questions asked.

The truth is, the marketing around trades is often outdated, uninspired, or completely missing. Compare that to the billion-dollar branding machine behind four-year colleges, and it's no wonder students aren't lining up for vocational pathways.

Universities spend millions on glossy brochures, viral social media campaigns, and celebrity endorsements. They paint pictures of campus life, lifelong friendships, and intellectual discovery. Meanwhile, trade schools often rely on basic job fair booths and outdated brochures that make the work look anything but appealing.

To fix it, we need a rebrand:

- **Show real people with real success stories,** not stock photos of people in hard hats, but actual tradespeople who own their homes, take vacations, and build successful lives.

- **Highlight the financial benefits:** no debt, high starting wages, and rapid advancement opportunities.

- **Showcase excellent benefits:** good health insurance, solid retirement plans, and job security that white-collar workers increasingly lack.

- **Make visible the pride, purpose, and professionalism** of skilled labor through authentic storytelling.

- Use the same storytelling power that sells sneakers and tech—to sell *respect*.

Reality Check: We're Not Just Competing With College

We're competing with culture.

We're up against viral videos, influencer fame, and a fast-paced world that glorifies instant gratification. It's not just about telling young people the trades matter; it's about showing them how.

Believe it or not, the trades are not technology-free. All kinds of technology are being used on job sites—from LiDAR to AutoCAD to hand-held devices for surveying, air monitoring, gas monitoring, and more. Someone must know how to apply those kinds of technologies in the field. In addition, drones are in use a lot now, too.

The modern construction site looks nothing like what most people imagine. Today's tradespeople use advanced software, operate sophisticated machinery, and solve complex technical problems. Even a dirt-work operator needs to know how to program his machine to keep and maintain a certain depth and speed to do the job. We need to show the reality, not outdated stereotypes.

Give them a reason to believe this path leads to meaning, freedom, and the future. Let them see a life where work isn't just tolerable; it's *badass*.

Cracking the Gen Z Code

Generation Z is the first generation to grow up entirely in the digital age, and that shapes how they consume information and make decisions. They have an attention span of about eight seconds for initial engagement (Microsoft, 2015), but don't mistake that for shallow thinking. They're more discriminating than previous generations; they just gather information differently.

A Gen Z job seeker might discover a trade through a 15-second TikTok video, but they'll immediately research the company, read employee reviews, check social media presence, and investigate career prospects before making any commitment. They're adept at leveraging brief content into comprehensive research.

This means our recruitment strategies need to be multilayered:

Platform-Specific Approaches

- **TikTok**: Short, authentic videos showing day-in-the-life content, behind-the-scenes footage, and real employee testimonials.

- **Instagram**: Visual storytelling with high-quality photos and stories showcasing projects and workplace culture.

- **LinkedIn**: Professional content highlighting career advancement and skills development.

- **YouTube**: Longer-form content diving deep into training programs and career paths.

Content That Resonates

- employee-generated content rather than corporate messaging

- behind-the-scenes look at daily work life

- success stories with concrete details about earnings and advancement

- technology integration and innovation in trades

- work-life balance and company values alignment

Start With Exposure

The trades can't just show up at job fairs and expect results. Exposure must start early. How many little kids don't love big trucks and construction equipment? And to be able to get up close to it, see it, touch it, and sit in the seat? It's exciting and often starts just that early. Therefore, keep that momentum and interest, and foster it throughout their school years.

Early Engagement Strategies

- **middle-school field trips** to training centers, farms of any kind or size, and active construction sites

- **skilled trades days** with hands-on demos where students can try welding, electrical work, or operating equipment

- **mentorship programs** that pair teens with working tradespeople for job shadowing and career guidance

- **social media campaigns** that speak their language and showcase the technology and innovation in modern trades

Parents need education. Teachers need resources. Schools need partnerships. And the trades need to show up—consistently, visibly, and with a message that resonates. To the uneducated, construction jobs are scary, but with the right training and safety in place, construction jobs are exciting and fulfilling.

Building Authentic Employer Brands

Generation Z values authenticity above almost everything else. They've grown up seeing through corporate marketing jargon, and they can spot inauthentic messaging from a mile away. For trades recruitment to succeed, we need to build genuine employer brands that reflect real workplace cultures and values.

Key Elements of Authentic Trades Branding

- **transparency about work conditions**—both challenges and rewards

- **real employee testimonials**—not scripted corporate videos

- **company values in action**—showing, not just stating, commitment to safety, training, and advancement

- **diversity and inclusion efforts**—demonstrating that the trades welcome everyone

- **technology integration**—highlighting how modern trades use cutting-edge tools and systems

Employee Advocacy Programs

Leverage existing employees, especially younger workers, as brand ambassadors. Their authentic experiences and social media presence can be far more powerful than any corporate marketing campaign. When a 25-year-old electrician posts about their new truck purchase or dream vacation funded by their trade work, it resonates with peers in ways traditional advertising never could.

The Role of Technology in Modern Recruitment

Today's recruitment landscape requires sophisticated digital strategies. With 79% of job seekers using social media to find jobs (*Why Job Seekers Rely on Social Media*, n.d.), and 88% of Millennials and 90% of Gen Z using social platforms (Shriber, 2023), a strong digital presence isn't optional; it's essential.

Targeted Digital Advertising

- Use data analytics to identify and target specific demographics.
- Create platform-specific content that leverages each channel's unique features.
- Implement mobile-optimized application processes—Gen Z expects seamless mobile experiences.
- Utilize artificial intelligence and automation for efficient candidate screening and engagement.

Multi-Channel Approach

Don't rely on a single platform or strategy. Generation Z gathers information from multiple sources before making decisions. Hence, your recruitment strategy should include:

- social media presence across multiple platforms
- company website with detailed career information
- employee review site management
- video content showcasing workplace culture
- interactive virtual tours and training previews

Measuring Success and Adapting

The key to successful Gen Z recruitment is agility. Social media trends move quickly, and what works today might be outdated next month. Therefore, successful recruitment strategies require the following:

Continuous Monitoring

- Track engagement metrics across all platforms.
- Monitor changes in candidate preferences and expectations.
- Stay current with social media trends and platform updates.
- Regularly survey new hires about their recruitment experience.

Adaptation and Innovation

- Be willing to experiment with new platforms and content types.
- Adjust messaging based on performance data.
- Incorporate feedback from successful recruits.
- Stay ahead of cultural and technological changes.

We're Not Just Building Things; We're Building Awareness

Recruitment isn't about filling seats in a training center; it's about changing minds, shifting perceptions, and opening doors.

The trades offer more than work. They offer purpose. They offer financial stability. They offer career growth. They offer the satisfaction of building something tangible and lasting. In addition, they offer job security in an uncertain world.

But you can't choose what you've never seen. That's our challenge and our opportunity.

We need to meet young people where they are—on their phones, on social media, in their digital spaces—and show them that the future of work isn't just in Silicon Valley or on Wall Street. It's in the skilled hands that build, maintain, and improve the physical world we all depend on.

Let's change that.

The future of the trades depends on more than tools and talent; it depends on telling the story right.

Chapter 5:
Craft, Honor, and Purpose

Some people work to get by, others work to make a name. And then, there are those who work with purpose—because what they do *matters*.

That's the heart of the skilled trade.

This chapter is about what keeps skilled workers coming back each day. It's not just the paycheck—though a solid one doesn't hurt. It's the *craft*. The *honor*. The knowledge that what you build today will stand tomorrow. And when the worst happens—when disasters strike, when the world needs rebuilding—it's the trades that answer the call without hesitation.

Craftsmanship Is a Calling

In the trades, you learn to see the details others overlook. The straightness of a weld. The flushness of a joint. The way a structure breathes when it's built right.

That's not just work; that's art. And the pride in doing it right runs deep.

We've grown used to mass production, disposable everything, and rush jobs, but in the trades, the best work isn't fast; it's *solid*. The best workers aren't rushed; they're *skilled*.

This dedication to quality over quantity sets tradespeople apart in a world increasingly focused on speed and efficiency at the expense of durability.

To choose a craft is to choose patience. Precision. Practice. It's a long game, and the reward isn't always flashy. Sometimes, it's just knowing a job won't have to be redone. That a family is safe in their home. That a powerline holds strong in a storm. That a bridge will carry traffic for decades to come.

The craftsperson understands something fundamental: True skill can't be rushed, automated, or shortcut. It must be earned through repetition, refined through experience, and passed down through mentorship. In an age of instant everything, this commitment to mastery becomes even more precious.

Honor in the Work

There's a quiet dignity in labor that doesn't beg for recognition.

You show up before sunrise. You leave after dark. You take pride in sweat, calluses, and the weight of a full day. And maybe no one notices what you did. But if you *didn't* do it, they'd notice real fast.

That's honor, not just in how you work, but in *what you're willing to work for*. Safety. Shelter. Power. Clean water. Stability. The things we all rely on, things taken for granted every day, built by people who rarely ask for a thank you.

This honor manifests in countless small moments: the electrician who stays late to restore power to a neighborhood, the welder who redoes a joint because it doesn't meet their standards, the carpenter who builds something to last generations, not just years. It's the understanding that your work affects real people in real ways and that responsibility is both humbling and motivating.

The honor in trades work comes from its fundamental necessity. While other industries might debate their value or contribution to society, tradespeople know without question that their work matters. Every building, every road, every piece of infrastructure exists because skilled hands made it real.

Reality Check: When the World Shut Down, the Trades Didn't

During the COVID-19 pandemic, millions were told to stay home. Offices closed. Schools shifted online. Entire industries ground to a halt. But the trades? They kept going. Construction crews, utility workers, building engineers, and maintenance techs showed up—in masks, in gloves, in uncertainty—to keep the world turning.

I was working as a safety professional when COVID hit. I was down for one week, not because the company was scared, but because, as a utility company, they needed to set a path forward for their employees. That was the only time I was down: I worked throughout the pandemic, traveled across the United States, and continued to work because, along with the trades, we were essential for the Nation to keep running.

The statistics tell the story of that essential nature. Construction was deemed essential in states across the country, recognizing that infrastructure couldn't wait for the pandemic to end. Note that nearly 1 million construction workers initially lost their jobs in the chaos of the early pandemic response, but by May 2020, construction showed strong job recovery, adding 464,000 jobs as the essential nature of the work became clear (*The Employment Situation*, 2020).

Brandon Mabile, a corporate business development director, put it perfectly: "The fact that construction was deemed essential likely saved the industry as we know it and kept hundreds of thousands of people employed. Had construction shut down, many skilled workers would have been forced to find new employment, and who knows how many would have returned to the industry when work finally resumed" (Phillips, 2025).

They weren't just essential in title; they were essential in *truth*. While many industries discovered they could function remotely or pause operations, the trades proved that some work simply cannot stop. Water treatment plants needed maintenance. Power lines required repair. Construction projects essential to public health and safety continued around the clock.

That moment stripped away pretense. We saw who keeps things running. And it wasn't the influencers or executives working from home; it was the people in hard hats, tool belts, and boots, working in conditions made more dangerous by an invisible threat, adapting safety protocols on the fly while maintaining the infrastructure that allowed everyone else to shelter in place.

Construction and utility workers across the country worked through the pandemic's most dangerous phases, often before adequate protective equipment was available (Centers for Disease Control and Prevention, 2021). They staggered shifts, maintained social distancing on job sites, and figured out how to do inherently collaborative work while keeping each other safe. Their sacrifice kept hospitals powered, water flowing, and essential infrastructure functioning when society needed it most.

The Ultimate Test: September 11, 2001

When the unthinkable happened on September 11, 2001, it was construction companies and tradesmen and women who showed up, right alongside the firefighters and first responders. They rolled in with excavators, dump trucks, cranes, and workers. On one of America's worst days in history, the men and women in construction did not hesitate; they left their projects and descended on the World Trade Center disaster in droves from all over the United States.

Not for glory or recognition, but because America needed them.

The numbers were staggering and humbling. By the end of the first week after the attacks, over 1,000 ironworkers from across North America had arrived to help, along with countless others (Smith et al., 2019). Construction work across New York City stopped when workers left their jobs to pitch in at Ground Zero. There was a huge need for ironworkers, welders, carpenters, electricians, and skilled operators to support the extensive recovery efforts.

More than 50,000 workers and volunteers responded to Ground Zero (*Why Weren't 9/11 Recovery Workers Protected*, 2007), working in conditions that defied description. They formed bucket brigades to move debris piece by piece. They cut through twisted steel beams with torches, carefully navigating a pile of wreckage that could shift and collapse at any moment. They worked 12-hour shifts in toxic dust and smoke, often without adequate respiratory protection, because the work was too important to wait for perfect safety conditions.

In this context, the Mohawk ironworkers' story is particularly powerful. These workers had built the Twin Towers in the first place—their grandfathers and uncles had helped construct them. When the towers fell, it wasn't just buildings collapsing; it was generations of their work and heritage. "When the towers went down," one observer noted, "it wasn't just buildings collapsing; it was also a great deal of personal history that went down with those towers" (Hill, 2001).

Yet they didn't hesitate. Mohawk ironworker Michael Mitchell worked daily at the site well into November. Brothers Paul and Peter Jacobs worked night shifts, walking through 6 in. of dust and debris, cutting paths so rescuers could safely navigate the wreckage. They compared the work to a massive game of Pick-up Sticks—move one thing, and something else would shift (Hill, 2001).

These workers understood something fundamental: When catastrophe strikes, it's not think tanks or consultants who rebuild America; it's the people who know how to move earth, cut steel, and make things work again. The same skills that build skyscrapers become the tools for recovery and hope.

Danny Doyle, one of the ironworkers who wielded cutting torches at Ground Zero, later recalled the moment that crystallized the honor of their work: "I remember coming out of the hole, and it was Fleet Week, and all the sailors and the enlisted men had come down, and they lined the whole ramp on both sides, and as we were leaving... they were all saluting us" (Stout et al., 2006).

The formal recovery operation concluded on May 30, 2002, with the ceremonial removal of the last 58-ft steel column from the site. That column, covered in a black shroud, was driven up a ramp to street level as construction workers, first responders, and families gathered to mark the end of one chapter and the beginning of another (New York City Office of Emergency Management, 2002).

The Health Cost of Heroism

The bravery and dedication of these workers came at a tremendous cost. Hundreds of thousands of tons of toxic debris containing more than 2,500 contaminants and known carcinogens were spread across Lower Manhattan when the towers collapsed (Sayantani, 2024). An estimated 18,000 people have developed illnesses as a result of exposure to the toxic dust (Shukman, 2011).

By 2018, at least 15 FBI agents had died from cancer due to their roles in the aftermath (Shortell & Kounang, 2018). Moreover, more than 2,000 first responders and others who were at Ground Zero have died due to 9/11-related illnesses (Feuer, 2018). According to the Uniformed Firefighters Association, about 1 in every 8 firefighters who worked at Ground Zero has been diagnosed with cancer (Hughes, 2018).

Construction workers, many of whom worked the longest shifts and were exposed to the worst conditions, continue to suffer from respiratory problems, cancer, and other health issues more than two decades later. Yet when asked, most say they would do it again. Because that's what the trades do: They show up when they're needed, regardless of the personal cost.

What You Build Builds You

There's pride in finishing a job right. In mentoring an apprentice. In knowing your skills *count*. Tradespeople walk a little taller—not from arrogance but from earned self-respect. Tradesmen and women don't boast about their accomplishments. They are quiet, behind the scenes, and proud.

The character forged in the trades extends far beyond job sites. The problem-solving skills developed from troubleshooting electrical systems translate to tackling any challenge. The patience learned from perfecting a weld teaches persistence in all areas of life. And most importantly, the teamwork required on construction sites builds leadership abilities that serve families and communities.

Physical work builds physical strength, but it also builds mental toughness. When you've worked through a brutal winter pouring concrete, climbed transmission towers in high winds, or welded in cramped spaces for hours, you develop a resilience that serves you everywhere. You learn that discomfort is temporary, that most problems have solutions, and that hard work almost always pays off.

The trades also build a unique perspective on value and durability. When you've built something with your own hands, you understand the difference between quality and flash, between substance and style. You appreciate things that last, work reliably, and were built right the first time.

A Legacy of Service

The essential nature of trades work extends far beyond individual projects or even major disasters. Every generation of tradespeople builds the foundation for the next. The bridges we drive across, the buildings we work in, and the power systems that run our lives are all a testament to skilled workers who take pride in their craft.

Modern tradespeople continue this tradition while adapting to new challenges. Climate change demands new approaches to construction and energy systems. Aging infrastructure requires innovative solutions for repair and replacement. Technology integration means today's electricians work with smart grids, and today's plumbers install high-efficiency systems monitored by sensors.

Yet the fundamental character remains unchanged: show up, do the work right, take care of your team, serve your community, and provide for your family. Whether it's restoring power after a storm, building homes for growing families, or responding to national tragedies, the trades embody a service ethic that keeps society functioning (*The Home Builders Institute*, 2024).

Recognition and Respect

The COVID-19 pandemic and other recent events have brought new recognition to essential workers, including those in the trades. But this recognition shouldn't be occasional or crisis-driven. The essential nature of skilled work deserves constant acknowledgment and respect.

Every flip of a light switch, turn of a faucet, or safe passage over a bridge represents skilled work done well. Every time we're warm in winter or cool in summer, we benefit from tradespeople who have installed and maintained those systems. Every time we don't think about infrastructure, it's because someone in the trades did their job right.

The honor in trades work isn't just about individual achievement; it's about being part of something larger. It's about building and maintaining the physical foundation of civilization. It's about ensuring that essential services continue, that people have safe places to live and work, and that communities can thrive.

The Continuing Call

Today, as infrastructure ages and new challenges emerge, the essential nature of trades work becomes even more critical. The next generation of tradespeople won't just maintain what exists; they'll build what's needed for the future. Smart cities, renewable energy systems, resilient infrastructure that can withstand climate change—all of it will be built by skilled hands guided by experienced minds.

The craftsperson's commitment to quality, the honor of essential work, and the willingness to serve when called upon aren't just nice ideas; they're the foundation of everything we depend on. They're what separates civilization from chaos, order from disorder, and safety from danger.

Because in the end, it's not just about what you build; it's about how it builds *you*—stronger, sharper, more capable than the day before. And it's about knowing that when the world needs rebuilding, when disasters strike, and when essential work must be done, the trades will answer the call.

The trades don't just build structures; they build character. And that makes them essential in more ways than one.

Chapter 6:

Skills That Aren't Learned in an Office

Not all education happens in a classroom. Some of the most valuable lessons you'll ever learn come from someone beside you, not in front of a whiteboard, but over a workbench.

The trades have always relied on this: the passing of skill from one set of hands to another. Father to daughter. Aunt to nephew. Journeyman to apprentice. Elder to eager kid with more questions than calluses.

This chapter is about where skills come from, not just formally, but *formatively*. Moreover, it's about a crisis we're facing: the loss of generations of accumulated wisdom as experienced workers retire, taking their knowledge with them.

As technology like the Internet of Things (IoT) becomes more prevalent on jobsites, hands-on skills still form the foundation (see Chapter 9 for more on tech in the trades).

Learning on the Home Front

Before training centers, before online certifications, and before HR onboarding videos, there was family. There was a community. There was the weekend project, the "hold this flashlight," the "come help me fix this."

That's where the spark was lit for many. Watching a grandparent change a belt on a mower. Helping mom with drywall patches. Being shown how to run a saw safely, or measure twice, cut once. Learning that tools have names, purposes, and proper respect.

We've moved so far away from that. We've forgotten how powerful it is. Young people used to learn by *doing*, not googling. They developed an intuitive understanding of how things work, how materials behave, and how solutions emerge from problems.

Now, some can't even name a tool, let alone use one. But that's not their fault. It's what happens when we remove hands-on learning from daily life. When we outsource every repair, replace instead of fix, and treat the physical world as someone else's problem.

The result is a generation that feels disconnected from real work—and unprepared to handle it. They've been raised in a world where everything is a service call away, where YouTube videos replace hands-on teaching, and where competence with physical objects is increasingly rare.

The Value of *Old School* Knowledge

There's no substitute for the kind of knowledge that comes from experience. The little tricks. The work-arounds. The "you won't find this in a book" wisdom that makes the difference between a job well done and one that barely gets by.

Tradespeople carry generations of that knowledge in their heads and hands, and when it's shared, it doesn't just teach skills; it builds *respect*. Because when an older hand shows a younger one how to do something right, it's more than just instruction. It's an investment. It's legacy work. It's the passing of *tribal knowledge*.

But here's the reality: The *old school* tradesperson doesn't automatically share knowledge or tricks. You have to earn that wisdom. You have to show up on time, every day. You have to show you want to learn the trade, and you have to work hard. When they see that drive, then they may show you a little trick that will make your day easier and the job less of a hardship.

However, some of them won't show you how to do anything as they don't want to lose their job to a younger worker; they don't want to become obsolete. It is a sad situation, really, because there is so much tribal knowledge that these members can bring to the work and to the younger members coming up in the trades.

And it matters more now than ever because we're facing an unprecedented knowledge crisis.

The Great Knowledge Crisis

We're living through what experts call the *Boomer Brain Drain*: the largest transfer of institutional knowledge in human history. By 2030, all 75 million baby boomers will be at least 65 years old (Stanley, 2023). Until then, approximately 10,000 boomers retire each day, taking decades of accumulated wisdom with them (Fry, 2020).

The numbers are staggering:

- Seventy-four million baby boomers are reaching retirement age. (*The Demographic Outlook*, 2024)

- Forty-seven percent of younger workers have been left to learn their jobs on their own when employers fail to manage knowledge transfer from retiring employees (*47% of U.S. Employees Forced to Self-Train*, 2022).

- Forty percent of companies lose specialized knowledge and expertise faster than they gain it (*Knowledge Sharing*, n.d.).

- Only 83% of employers report having significant numbers of baby boomers at or approaching retirement age, yet most have no formal knowledge transfer plan (Gwoke, n.d.).

In the skilled trades, this crisis is particularly acute. These workers possess decades of experience with a deep understanding of processes, equipment, and techniques that often aren't written down anywhere. They know the quirks of specific machines, the work-arounds for common problems, and the subtle indicators that something needs attention before it fails catastrophically.

This is *tribal knowledge*: the unwritten information that is not commonly known by others but is needed to accomplish quality work. It includes:

- machine setup and maintenance techniques not in the official manuals

- troubleshooting methods for specific equipment problems

- efficiency hacks and work-arounds developed over the years

- supplier and material insights about what works best in real conditions

- safety knowledge gained from experience with dangerous situations

When skilled workers retire or leave, this knowledge often goes with them, leading to costly disruptions, decreased productivity, and knowledge gaps that take significant time and resources to fill.

The Mentorship Solution

The solution to the knowledge crisis isn't just documentation; it's mentorship. Formal apprenticeship programs that include structured mentoring components experience significantly higher success rates. For example in Ontario, in this setting, 83% of apprentices with mentors report that they wouldn't have succeeded without them, and 92% learned unique insights from their mentors that weren't available anywhere else (FTI Ontario, 2024).

Effective mentorship in the trades involves more than just teaching technical skills. Mentors fill many roles: teacher, guide, counselor, advisor, motivator, coach, role model, door opener, and referral agent. And not just about the job, but about Life in general. They provide:

- Technical knowledge transfer: Hands-on training that goes beyond classroom instruction, allowing apprentices to learn by doing and applying theoretical knowledge in practical situations.

- Industry wisdom: Insights into industry standards, best practices, and emerging trends that aren't found in textbooks or training manuals.

- Professional development: Guidance on navigating workplace dynamics, understanding employer expectations, and building successful careers.

- Problem-solving skills: Real-world experience in handling unexpected challenges, equipment failures, and complex troubleshooting situations.

- Safety knowledge: Critical understanding of hazards, risk assessment, and safety protocols learned through years of experience.

The Apprenticeship Model

Modern apprenticeship programs recognize the critical importance of mentorship. In FY 2021, more than 241,000 new apprentices entered the national apprenticeship system, with over 593,000 apprentices obtaining skills while earning wages (*FY 2021 Data*, 2021). These programs typically involve

- **eighty percent on-the-job training,** working alongside experienced professionals

- **twenty percent classroom instruction,** covering theoretical knowledge and safety protocols

- **structured mentorship relationships** with *journeypersons* who guide skill development

- **progressive skill-building** with documented progress and competency assessments

- **earn-while-you-learn models** that provide financial stability during training

The most successful programs include formal mentor training that teaches *journeypersons* how to effectively transfer knowledge. This training acknowledges their expertise while teaching them about different learning styles and how to structure instruction based on individual needs.

A New Kind of Apprenticeship

The evolution of apprenticeship programs shows how hands-on learning continues to adapt and expand. When people think of *apprenticeship*, they typically picture someone learning to weld, frame, or wire. But innovative programs are proving that the apprenticeship model works for emerging specializations within the trades.

Take Washington State's Certified Safety Specialist Apprenticeship, a trailblazing program that proves blue-collar careers don't stop at the tools. This state-registered apprenticeship trains individuals to become safety professionals—people responsible for making sure job sites run without injury, loss, or shortcuts.

It's not a corporate desk job. It's not a fallback. It's a field-tested, boots-on-ground role that ensures others make it home safe.

Apprentices earn while they learn, taking classes through Edmonds College while working in the field. After about 2 years and 4,500 hours of combined training, they graduate as journey-level Certified Safety Specialists (Standards of Apprenticeship, 2019). That title comes with real weight—and real pay.

This program demonstrates several key principles that make modern apprenticeships successful:

- Practical application: Safety apprentices learn by being on actual job sites, understanding real hazards, and developing solutions to actual problems rather than theoretical scenarios.

- Mentorship integration: Experienced safety professionals guide apprentices through complex situations, teaching them not just regulations but the judgment needed to apply them effectively.

- Industry relevance: The program responds to real industry needs—every construction site needs qualified safety professionals, and this creates a clear career pathway.

- Skill evolution: It shows how traditional trades knowledge evolves into specialized roles that still require hands-on expertise and field experience.

This program is proof that blue-collar work keeps evolving. The world needs people who can build, but also people who know how to keep the builders safe. The apprenticeship model adapts to meet these needs while maintaining its core strength: learning by doing under the guidance of those who've mastered the craft.

This isn't a backup plan; it's another path forward, one that demonstrates how apprenticeship programs continue to create new opportunities while preserving the fundamental value of hands-on learning and mentorship.

When I changed careers in 2004, I was still working with my tools but taking online safety classes at Indiana University, Bloomington, IN. I was a lot older than my classmates, but I was able to explain how the world worked when applying safety.

Construction safety was a natural fit for me; I had been working with my tools for 14 years by the time I graduated in 2008. I left the Ironworkers right before graduation and had a full-time safety job right after graduation. I had some bumps starting out, but because I could talk the talk of the construction worker, I was able to garner respect from some of the most hardcore "I don't do safety" tradesmen out there.

Overall, my time in the trades has served me well over the years.

Challenges in Knowledge Transfer

Despite the critical importance of mentorship, significant challenges exist in effectively transferring knowledge between generations:

- Mentor preparedness: Many experienced workers lack formal training in teaching or mentoring techniques. Apprentices often report that their mentors don't understand apprenticeship requirements or how to effectively transfer knowledge.

- Communication barriers: Different generations have different communication preferences and learning styles. Boomers prefer face-to-face or phone communication (*Generational Communication*, n.d.), while younger workers are more comfortable with digital platforms.

- Reluctance to share: Some experienced workers are hesitant to share their knowledge, fearing it might make them replaceable or reduce their value to the organization.

- Time constraints: Effective knowledge transfer takes time, but production pressures often leave little room for thorough teaching and learning.

- Documentation challenges: Much tribal knowledge is intuitive and difficult to document in traditional written formats.

Modern Solutions for Ancient Wisdom

Organizations are developing innovative approaches to capture and transfer tribal knowledge:

- Video documentation: Using YouTube-style videos to document processes, as many younger workers learn better from visual demonstrations than written instructions (Freifeld, 2023).

- Mentorship programs: Formal pairing of experienced workers with newcomers, including structured goals, regular meetings, and progress tracking.

- Cross-training initiatives: Ensuring multiple people can perform essential functions, which reduces dependence on single individuals.

- Reverse mentoring: Programs where younger workers teach technology skills to experienced workers in exchange for learning traditional techniques.

- Exit interviews and knowledge capture: Systematic processes for documenting expertise before experienced workers retire.

- Apprenticeship enhancement: Strengthening formal apprenticeship programs with better mentor training and support systems.

Reality Check: We've Outsourced Too Much

We live in an age where we can order anything, replace everything, and google the rest. But convenience has a cost: We've lost our baseline competence. We've lost the confidence that comes with knowing how to fix, build, adjust, and *understand* the physical world.

The result? A generation that feels disconnected from real work—and unprepared to handle it. This disconnection has real consequences:

- decreased problem-solving skills when faced with physical challenges

- reduced confidence in handling tools and equipment
- lost understanding of how everyday objects work
- increased dependence on specialists for basic repairs and maintenance
- diminished appreciation for skilled manual work

We don't just need to restore shop class; we need to restore *trust in our capability*. And that starts at home, with simple projects and basic skills that build confidence and competence.

The Role of Technology in Knowledge Transfer

Modern technology offers new opportunities for preserving and transferring tribal knowledge:

- Digital platforms: Connected worker platforms that can capture and share real-time knowledge from experienced workers.
- Augmented reality: Systems that can overlay instructions directly onto the user's view of the task at hand (Augmented Reality, 2025).
- Artificial intelligence: Tools that can analyze patterns in expert decision-making and help transfer that knowledge to newer workers.
- Mobile applications: Platforms that allow easy documentation and sharing of tips, tricks, and troubleshooting guides.
- Videoconferencing: Technology that enables remote mentoring and expert consultation even when experienced workers aren't physically present.

Building a Culture of Knowledge Sharing

Successful knowledge transfer requires more than just tools and programs; it requires a culture that values and rewards sharing expertise:

- Recognition programs: Acknowledging and rewarding employees who actively contribute to knowledge-sharing initiatives.

- Leadership support: Management must actively support and participate in knowledge transfer efforts, demonstrating their importance to the organization.

- Structured relationships: Formal mentoring relationships with clear goals, expectations, and support systems.

- Continuous learning: Environments where experienced and new workers are encouraged to learn from each other.

- Documentation support: Providing tools and time for workers to document their knowledge and expertise.

Mentorship Isn't Just for the Union Hall

Mentorship can happen on the jobsite or at the kitchen table. It can be formal or off-the-cuff. However, it always starts with someone *willing to teach* and someone *open to learning*. It may be the noisy neighbor kid who is always hanging around. Take that opportunity to teach them something; you never know where it will lead.

The most effective mentorship often happens in informal settings:

- weekend projects where skills are taught naturally

- repair tasks that become learning opportunities

- community projects that bring generations together

- family traditions of working with hands and tools

- neighborhood relationships where knowledge is shared freely

If you've got skills, pass them on. If you don't, ask to learn. Because the trades are more than a paycheck; they're a heritage. And every time we teach someone how to work with their hands, we're not just filling a skills gap; we're building confidence, pride, and independence.

The Multigenerational Opportunity

The current workforce challenge also presents an opportunity. With four generations working together—baby boomers, Generation X, millennials, and Generation Z—there's unprecedented potential for knowledge exchange:

- **Baby boomers** bring decades of experience, institutional knowledge, and proven problem-solving techniques.

- **Generation X** serves as a bridge between older and younger workers, understanding both traditional methods and modern technology.

- **Millennials** offer fresh perspectives, collaborative approaches, and comfort with digital tools for knowledge sharing.

- **Generation Z** brings digital nativity, adaptability, and new approaches to learning and communication.

The key is creating structured opportunities for these generations to learn from each other, combining the wisdom of experience with the innovation of youth.

The Future of Skilled Learning

As we look ahead, the most successful trade organizations will be those that master the art of knowledge transfer. This means:

- investing in formal mentorship programs with trained mentors
- using technology to capture and share tribal knowledge
- creating cultures where knowledge sharing is valued and rewarded
- building bridges between generations of workers
- recognizing that learning is a lifelong process for everyone

The alternative—losing generations of accumulated wisdom as experienced workers retire—is too costly to accept. The tribal knowledge held by today's skilled workers represents centuries of collective learning, innovation, and problem-solving that cannot simply be replaced by reading manuals or watching videos.

Personal Responsibility

Every skilled worker has a responsibility to pass on what they've learned. Every apprentice has a responsibility to seek out mentorship and value the wisdom of experience. Every organization has a responsibility to create systems that facilitate effective knowledge transfer.

But the responsibility extends beyond formal programs. It's about recognizing that knowledge sharing is fundamental to the survival and growth of the trades. It's about understanding that the techniques you've mastered, the shortcuts you've discovered, and the wisdom you've gained through experience are too valuable to lose.

When an experienced *tradesperson* teaches a younger worker the right way to do something—not just the way that works, but the way that works best—they're not just transferring skills; they're preserving traditions, maintaining standards, and ensuring that the next generation can build on what came before rather than starting from scratch.

> *Not every skill can be taught in an office. Some are passed down tool to tool and hand to hand, one honest lesson at a time.*

Chapter 7:

Danger, Risk, and Pride—The Mental Weight of the Trades

There's a toughness to the trades, but it's not just physical. It's mental. Emotional. Psychological.

This chapter dives into the hidden weight tradespeople carry: the daily risks, the long-term strain, and the quiet pride that holds it all together.

Because under every tool belt slung over a shoulder, there's a burden you don't always see. A sick child, a loss of a parent or spouse, a divorce, college tuition, missing an important school event or game you promised you'd be at... It's all there in every worker who shows up, carrying not just tools but the full weight of life's responsibilities and pressures.

It's Not Just Hard Work; It's Hazardous Work

Jobs in the trades are some of the most dangerous in the workforce. Falls, electrocutions, heavy equipment accidents, heat stress, and trench collapses aren't rare occurrences but real, daily risks that define the working environment.

The statistics paint a sobering picture. According to the U.S. Bureau of Labor Statistics, construction had 1,075 fatalities in 2023, the highest number since 2011, accounting for nearly 1 in 5 workplace deaths nationwide (Phillips, 2024). That means a worker dies every 99 minutes from a work-related injury, and 1 in 5 of those deaths happens on a construction site.

The fatal injury rate for construction workers is 9.6 deaths per 100,000 full-time workers, higher than the nationwide average, but also lower than the rate of 4.2 a year prior (Phillips, 2024). But these numbers only tell part of the story. They don't count the close calls, the life-changing injuries, and the accidents that leave workers permanently disabled but alive.

The Main Killer

Falls remain the leading killer, accounting for 39.2% (421) of all construction fatalities. Most fatal falls—64.4%—occur from heights between 6 and 30 feet. Portable ladders and stairs alone account for 109 construction deaths annually. Transportation incidents claim another 240 lives each year, while electrocutions account for 8% of fatalities, and caught-in/between accidents for 2% (The Safety Sentinel, 2025; *National Census*, 2024).

The human cost extends beyond individual tragedies. The total economic impact of construction-related injuries and fatalities reaches *$11.5 billion annually*, with the average cost per medically consulted injury estimated at $40,000 and the cost per fatality at $1.39 million (Clark, 2025).

Every day, workers step onto job sites knowing what's at stake. They double-check harnesses, spot for each other, and take the extra minute to do it safely. Because one mistake isn't just inconvenient; it can be fatal. That kind of awareness wears on you, and it deserves to be acknowledged.

Because in the back of every worker's mind is "what will my family do if I don't come home?"

Construction jobs are stressful for everyone—not just the managers dealing with clients, but also for the workers who are trying to accomplish what the manager promised the client they could do. Having been in the trades, we all try to make the foreman and the company look good, which brings the possibility of more assignments and being called back to work for that company again.

The Silent Epidemic: Mental Health in Construction

While physical dangers get most of the attention, there's another crisis killing construction workers at an alarming rate—one that's harder to see but just as deadly. Mental health challenges in construction have reached epidemic proportions, with suicide rates that dwarf even the high rates of workplace accidents.

The numbers are staggering and heartbreaking:

- More than 5,000 construction workers take their own lives each year—five times the number who die from job-related accidents (Ridderbusch, 2025).

- The construction industry has one of the highest suicide rates, coming in second overall. In 2021, 56 out of every 100,000 male construction workers took their own lives (Travelers, n.d.).

- This rate is four times higher than the national average and almost six times the rate of all construction fatalities combined.

Furthermore, a 2020 study found that 83% of construction workers have experienced a mental health issue (Mental Health, 2025). Almost half of construction workers have experienced symptoms of both anxiety and depression, a rate higher than that of the general U.S. population. Less than 5% of construction workers say they've consulted a mental health professional, while the figure for all U.S. adults is 22% (Ridderbusch, 2025).

The Mental Weight Nobody Talks About

There's pride in showing up, but there's also pressure. The kind of pressure that builds day after day, year after year, until it becomes almost unbearable:

- **to perform under stress** in dangerous conditions where mistakes can be fatal

- **to provide for a family** in an industry with seasonal work and economic uncertainty

- **to not let the crew down** when your teammates depend on you for their safety

- **to get it right, even when you're tired or hurting** from long hours and physical demands

- **to maintain the tough, stoic image** that the culture expects, never showing vulnerability

Mental health challenges are real in the trades, but they're rarely discussed. We're taught to push through, shake it off, and tough it out. The construction industry culture often values *toughness* in ways that discourage seeking help for mental health issues. Hence, many workers suffer in silence due to cultural expectations, feeling forced to deal with it rather than seeking the help they need.

That toughness comes at a cost. Subsequently, depression, anxiety, burnout, alcoholism, and substance abuse rates are significantly higher among construction and skilled labor workers than in many other sectors. Therefore, the industry exhibits what experts call a "perfect storm" of suicide risk factors.

Understanding the Risk Factors

Construction workers face a unique combination of risk factors that contribute to mental health challenges:

Demographic Factors

- To start with, around 90% of construction workers in the U.S. are men, and this group tends to have a higher risk of suicide (Travelers, n.d.).

- Plus, more than 15% of veterans, who face a 50% higher suicide rate, join the construction field, making up a significant part of the workforce (Travelers, n.d.)

- Many workers come from backgrounds with limited access to mental health resources.

Cultural Factors

- The stoic, self-reliant characteristics valued in construction reduce the likelihood that workers seek help when needed.

- Mental health issues and suicide remain taboo subjects on jobsites.

- There's often a stigma associated with appearing *weak* or unable to handle the job.

Work-Related Stressors

- **seasonal unemployment** and irregular work patterns that affect financial stability

- **long, irregular hours** that disrupt sleep patterns and family relationships

- **high psychological demands** and pressure to perform in dangerous conditions

- **low job control** and frequent changes in coworkers and tasks, as jobs change

- **work-family conflict** that strains relationships and creates guilt about missed family events

- **job insecurity** and the constant pressure to find the next project

Physical Health Impacts

- **chronic pain** from physically demanding work and higher rates of musculoskeletal disorders

- **sleep deprivation** from irregular schedules and demanding physical labor

- **higher rates of opioid use** to manage pain, leading to an increased risk of addiction

- **workplace injuries** that can end careers and create financial hardship

Substance Use Issues

- **higher rates of binge drinking** and heavy alcohol use compared to other industries

- **increased use of nonprescription opioids** and other drugs

- **substance abuse** as a form of self-medication for untreated mental health issues

The Compound Effect

These factors don't exist in isolation; they compound each other, creating a downward spiral that can be difficult to escape. A worker dealing with chronic back pain might start using opioids to manage the discomfort. The irregular work schedule strains his marriage, leading to arguments about missed family events. Financial pressure from seasonal layoffs creates additional stress. The combination of physical pain, relationship problems, financial stress, and substance use creates a perfect storm for a mental health crisis.

Evidence from the 2007–2009 financial crisis suggests that economic uncertainty can increase suicide risk in the construction industry (Milner et al., 2013). In addition, the COVID-19 pandemic only intensified these challenges as it brought job insecurity, health fears, and social isolation—all factors that can worsen existing mental health conditions.

Warning Signs and Recognition

Despite the taboo nature of mental health discussions in construction, there are observable warning signs that supervisors and coworkers can learn to recognize:

Behavioral Changes

- isolation, sitting alone at lunch, not talking with anyone
- increased absenteeism or tardiness
- decreased job performance or attention to safety protocols
- increased irritability or anger outbursts
- changes in personal hygiene or appearance

Physical Signs

- fatigue or exhaustion beyond normal work-related tiredness

- unexplained injuries or increased accident-prone behavior
- signs of substance use or impairment
- dramatic weight loss or gain

Emotional Indicators

- expressions of hopelessness or feeling trapped
- talking about feeling like a burden to others
- mentioning thoughts of death or suicide
- sudden mood swings or dramatic personality changes
- giving away personal possessions

Breaking the Silence

The construction industry is beginning to recognize that addressing mental health isn't just about compassion; it's essential for safety and productivity. Organizations like the Construction Industry Alliance for Suicide Prevention (CIASP) and the Associated General Contractors of America are leading efforts to reduce stigma and provide resources.

Some companies are implementing innovative approaches:

- **Mental Health First Aid Training** for supervisors to recognize warning signs and provide initial support until professional help can be obtained.
- **Peer Support Programs** that leverage the natural camaraderie of construction crews, training workers to support each other through difficult times.

- **Regular Safety Stand-Downs** that include mental health topics alongside traditional safety training, normalizing conversations about psychological well-being.

- **Employee Assistance Programs** that provide confidential counseling services and resources for workers and their families.

- **Toolbox Talks** that address stress management, work-life balance, and mental health resources as part of regular safety meetings.

Reality Check: Asking for Help Isn't Weakness

The strongest thing a *tradesperson* can do might not be lifting something heavy; it might be picking up the phone.

When I was still on my tools, I started having debilitating social anxiety and depression. The latter started when I was getting laid off from work a lot; there just weren't any jobs around at the time. In addition, social anxiety made it difficult for me to function, like going to the grocery store, working out of town, etc. People I was close to at work noticed, and mental health issues were not brought up on the job. You suffered in silence. I sought help on my own. Back then, there were not many resources available, and none existed on the job. Now, there is help to be had.

If you're struggling, you're not alone. And you're not broken. The challenges you face are real, and they're shared by thousands of other workers who understand exactly what you're going through.

You can call or text the *988 Suicide & Crisis Lifeline* or visit 988lifeline.org. It's free. It's confidential. It's 24-7. You've got backup. Always.

Additional Resources

- **OSHA Mental Health Resources:** Available at osha.gov/preventingsuicides

- **Construction Industry Alliance for Suicide Prevention:** constructionsuicideprevention.com

- **National Alliance on Mental Illness:** nami.org

- **Veterans Crisis Line:** 988, Press 1

The Path Forward

Addressing the mental health crisis in construction requires a fundamental shift in how the industry views and talks about psychological well-being.

This means:

- **creating safe spaces** for honest conversations about mental health challenges without fear of job loss or stigma

- **training leaders** to recognize warning signs and respond appropriately, and knowing when to listen and when to refer workers to professional help

- **normalizing help-seeking** by sharing stories of workers who have successfully addressed mental health challenges and returned to productive careers

- **addressing root causes** by examining work practices, schedules, and cultures that contribute to mental health problems

- **building support networks** that connect workers with resources, peer support, and professional mental health services

Risk Meets Reward

With danger comes pride. The kind of pride that says, "I built that." The kind that comes from knowing the job is hard and doing it anyway.

Tradespeople don't seek medals. However, there's deep satisfaction in knowing you've faced risk, managed it, and still created something real. There's pride in walking by a building and knowing you've helped raise its steel frame, flipping a light switch and remembering running that electrical circuit, and driving over a bridge and recalling the concrete you poured for its foundation.

It's a mix of respect for the danger and pride in the discipline. The knowledge that you've mastered skills that matter, that you've contributed to something lasting and important. Acknowledging the mental and emotional challenges of the work does not diminish that pride—if anything, it makes the accomplishment more meaningful.

The workers who seek help for mental health challenges aren't weak; they demonstrate the same courage and practical problem-solving approach that make them good at their trades. They recognize a problem and take action to fix it, just like they would with any other safety hazard on a jobsite.

Building a Culture of Care

The future of construction safety must include mental health as a core component. Just as the industry has made tremendous strides in reducing physical injuries through better safety protocols, training, and equipment, it can make similar progress in protecting workers' mental health.

This means creating work environments where:

- Mental health is discussed as openly as any other safety topic.

- Workers feel safe seeking help without fear of job loss or discrimination.

- Supervisors are trained to recognize and respond to mental health challenges.

- Resources are readily available and well-publicized.

- Success is measured not just by avoiding accidents but by supporting total worker well-being.

The same qualities that make someone good at construction work—attention to detail, problem-solving skills, teamwork, and perseverance—are exactly what's needed to address mental health challenges. The industry that built America's infrastructure has the strength and ingenuity to protect its most valuable resource: the people who do the work.

The job is hard. The risks are real. But the pride? That's what makes it all worth it. And getting help when you need it, that's not giving up on pride. That's protecting it.

Chapter 8:
Fixing the Pipeline—Schools, Parents, and Policy

The shortage of skilled labor isn't a mystery; it's the result of decades of misdirection.

We didn't just lose workers; we *lost the way to work*.

This chapter looks at the pipeline into the trades and the cracks that need fixing, starting with education, awareness, and the role families and leaders play in rebuilding the path.

Because the crisis we're facing didn't happen overnight, and it won't be solved overnight. However, it can be solved if we have the courage to challenge the assumptions that got us here and the wisdom to build something better.

Schools That Stopped Teaching Trades

For generations, high school shop classes gave students a taste of real-world work. Welding, woodworking, mechanics, and electrical basics—skills they could use or build a future on. These programs were more than just courses; they were pathways to middle-class prosperity and essential contributors to the skilled workforce that built America.

But as college prep took over, those programs disappeared at an alarming rate. The statistics tell a devastating story:

The Systematic Dismantling

- Between 1982 and 1992, while total high school credits increased by 11% and academic credits rose by 22%, vocational credits declined by *17%* (U.S. Department of Education, 1994).

- By 1992, vocational coursework made up only *16% of total coursework* completed by high school graduates, down from *21% in 1982* (National Center for Education Statistics, 1994).

- Since 1985, federal funding for vocational programs has *dropped by 32%* (Kreisman & Stange, 2025).

- Between 1990 and 2009, the number of vocational credits dropped by *14%*, or roughly 2/3 of a year of vocational studies (Gray & Herr, 2006).

By 2020, fewer than 10% of U.S. high schools offered robust vocational training (*The State of Career Technical Education*, 2020), and many of the remaining programs were underfunded or treated like academic leftovers—places to put students who *couldn't handle* real academics.

That's not just a missed opportunity; it's a systemic failure. Those kids who don't excel in the classroom and are barely passing? Get them in a shop, give them a wrench, and they will ace the work—they will be able to teach their classmates what they know. Give another kid a hammer and a plank of wood, and you will not believe what they can make you. Some kids are not built to thrive in a college classroom. Those kids need an outlet for their creativity, too.

The irony is profound: While schools eliminated hands-on learning opportunities, the demand for skilled workers continued to grow. Today's technological advances haven't replaced the need for skilled trades; they've made them more sophisticated and better-paying than ever.

The Academic–Vocational Caste System

The elimination of shop classes represents something deeper than budget cuts or space constraints; it reflects what education experts call the *academic–vocational caste system*: the pervasive belief that working with your mind is inherently superior to working with your hands (Rosenbaum, 2001).

This caste system has devastating consequences:

For Students

Those who might thrive in hands-on learning are left feeling as if they were misfits, academic failures, or less intelligent than their college-bound peers. Their natural talents go undiscovered and undeveloped.

For Schools

Institutions lose the ability to serve the full spectrum of students' talents and interests, creating narrow definitions of success that don't reflect real-world needs.

For Society

We've created a massive skills gap, with millions of high-paying jobs unfilled while students accumulate debt in fields with limited job prospects.

Viewing vocational programs as second-rate is one of the most corrosive problems in modern education (Gray & Herr, 2006). It forces a false choice between academic excellence and practical competence, when the reality is that both are essential and complementary.

The College-For-All Myth

The push toward universal college attendance, while well-intentioned, has created unrealistic expectations and unsustainable debt burdens. Recent data reveals the cracks in this approach:

- *Fifty-seven percent of college students* now agree that higher education is no longer *worth the cost* (Fishman et al., 2021).

- The average cost of a 4-year degree has reached *$127,000*, compared to *$33,000* for complete vocational training (College Board Advocacy and Access Communities, 2023).

- College tuition has increased by 181.3% over the past 20 years, with an average annual increase of 5.5% (Hanson, 2024).

- Moreover, *22% of college students* take up to 6 years to complete a 4-year degree, paying up to 150% of the degree's stated value (Marcus, 2021).

Meanwhile, students who might flourish in skilled trades are being pushed toward academic paths that don't suit their interests, abilities, or career goals. Parents and educators continue to push toward college because it's perceived as the *safe* choice, but this one-size-fits-all approach is failing both students and the economy.

The Economic Reality Check

The financial arguments for skilled trades have never been stronger:

Trade School Advantages

- Tuition increases at *half the rate* of four-year institutions (*Trends in College Pricing*, 2023).

- Students typically graduate debt-free or with minimal debt.

- Immediate employment opportunities are available upon completion.

Career Prospects

- Many skilled trades offer starting salaries of *$50,000+*.

- Advanced positions can reach six-figure incomes.

- Job security is available in essential, non-outsourceable work.

- There are opportunities for entrepreneurship and business ownership.

The *tool belt generation* is catching on to these realities. Gen Z is choosing trade schools over traditional universities at increasing rates, recognizing that crushing debt and uncertain job prospects aren't worth the prestige of a college degree.

Parents Who Mean Well but Miss the Mark

Every parent wants success for their kid. But when *success* only looks like a degree, a desk, and a 401(k), we limit our children without meaning to. However, some trades workers are quite millionaires—that annuity they have paid into since they were 18 years old is doing really well; they were able to pay off their mortgage early, retire from the trades at 55 years old, and have a second career—maybe as a teacher or a shop mechanic. On the other hand, the office worker is still trying to pay off that mortgage and put away a 401(k) retirement, but they must also work tirelessly until the retirement age of 67 nowadays.

Many parents simply don't know how rewarding trade careers can be. They hear *plumber* and think dirty work, not six-figure potential. They hear *welder* and picture sparks, not certifications, travel, or union security. They see construction sites and imagine danger and instability, not the steady work building the infrastructure that powers our economy.

The Information Gap Is Real

Parents often base their career advice on outdated stereotypes and incomplete information. They may know that their neighbor's kid graduated from college but is struggling to find work, while missing the fact that the electrician down the street just bought a new truck and took his family to Europe.

The Prestige Trap

Our culture has created artificial hierarchies that value credentials over competence and degrees over demonstrated skill. Parents feel social pressure to have a child who *went to college*, even when that path doesn't align with the child's interests or the economy's needs.

It's not about convincing every student to enter the trades; it's about making sure those *who would love it* hear about it. It's about expanding our definition of success to include the satisfaction of building something lasting, the security of essential skills, and the pride of honest work well done.

I can remember as a child watching my grandfather welding in the garage, fixing the old tractor, and building something others couldn't afford to buy—he had the parts and pieces to build whatever it was he wanted. That image of competence, creativity, and self-reliance left a lasting impression. Too many kids today never get those experiences.

Policy That Prioritizes College Over Competence

State and federal funding tends to follow traditional academic metrics: test scores, college enrollment rates, and graduation percentages.

Schools are rewarded for sending kids to college, not for preparing them for careers that don't require degrees.

But if we want to solve the labor crisis, policy must follow *need*. That means fundamentally restructuring how we fund, measure, and incentivize career preparation.

Current Federal Investment

The Perkins Act represents the primary federal investment in career and technical education, providing approximately *$1.4 billion annually* to states (Office of Career, Technical, and Adult Education, n.d.). The Strengthening Career and Technical Education for the 21st Century Act (Perkins V), signed in 2018, reauthorized this funding through 2024 and introduced important reforms:

- greater state flexibility in program design and implementation

- emphasis on work-based learning and industry partnerships

- focus on programs that lead to high-skill, high-wage, or in-demand occupations

- improved data collection and accountability measures

However, this investment pales in comparison to higher education funding. Federal Pell Grant expenditures, though declining over time, still amounted to $27.2 billion in 2022–23—nearly 20 times the Perkins investment (Ma and Pender, 2023).

What Policy Change Looks Like

- **expanding funding for vocational programs** to match the scale of workforce need

- **incentivizing schools to offer hands-on career training** through performance metrics that value career readiness alongside college readiness

- **creating scholarships and grants for apprenticeships** that rival those available for traditional college attendance

- **making labor pathways as visible and supported as academic ones** in guidance counseling, career fairs, and graduation requirements

In light of the aforementioned, we don't need to dismantle college; we need to *balance the scales*. This isn't about bashing colleges or the students who choose that route; this is about providing the same visibility to the trades for students who are not inclined to keep going to school.

The Personal Journey

I went to college right out of high school because that's what you did. As I stated earlier in the book, that career choice did not work out for me. I worked in the trades for 14 years and then returned to school to earn my bachelor's degree in safety management. I couldn't do the job anymore, but I wanted to be able to still work in construction. Safety kind of chose me at that point. I was way older than my classmates, but I was able to teach them about the real world and what they would be facing, and they helped me pass chemistry!

I have never regretted that choice. I still work in construction, but my experience in the trades serves me well even in safety. I can speak their language and help them see why they can't *do it that way*. I help them go home to their families; I know firsthand how someone getting hurt on the job affects not just the home family, but the work family, too.

This experience illustrates an important point: There's no shame in changing paths, and the skills learned in the trades often transfer to other careers in unexpected and valuable ways.

The problem isn't that some people choose college and others choose trades; it's that we've created artificial barriers that prevent people from exploring both options and making informed decisions.

Reality Check: The Digital Generation Isn't Hopeless

Yes, kids today spend hours on screens. Yes, fewer know how to use a wrench than a smartphone. But that doesn't mean they can't learn; it means we need to meet them where they are, then hand them a tool.

The *tool belt generation* proves that young people are hungry for meaningful work that offers financial security and personal satisfaction. Data from the National Student Clearinghouse Research Center shows that enrollment in vocational-focused community colleges increased 16% from 2022 to 2023, even as traditional college enrollment declined (*Term Enrollment Estimates*, 2023).

Modern Recruitment Strategies

- **Bring trades into social media:** Use TikTok, Instagram, and YouTube to showcase real-life success stories on platforms young people use.

- **Partner with influencers:** Work with content creators who can authentically speak to the benefits of skilled trades.

- **Virtual reality experiences:** Let students experience what it's like to operate heavy equipment or work on a construction site through VR.

- **Gaming integrations:** Partner with popular games that involve building and construction to introduce real-world applications.

- **Show real financial outcomes:** Provide concrete data about earnings, benefits, and career progression.

Give them reasons to believe they can make money, make a life, and make a difference in this field. Don't shame them for their digital habits; show them how those skills can complement hands-on work in an increasingly technology-integrated trades environment.

The Technology Integration Opportunity

Modern trades increasingly integrate advanced technology, making them more appealing to digitally-native young people:

Construction Technology

- Building Information Modeling (BIM) and 3D design software
- drone surveying and inspection
- augmented reality for project visualization
- IoT sensors for equipment monitoring
- robotic assistance in manufacturing and assembly

Require Workers

These technologies require workers who can:

- operate sophisticated software and hardware
- interpret complex data and digital models
- integrate traditional craftsmanship with cutting-edge tools
- adapt to rapidly evolving technological capabilities

This technological sophistication dispels outdated stereotypes about trades being *low-tech* or *backward*. Today's tradespeople are technological professionals who happen to work with their hands.

As the trades evolve with tools like the Internet of Things (IoT), we must teach young workers how to use both a wrench and a wireless monitor (see Chapter 9 for more information).

Building Comprehensive Solutions

Fixing the pipeline requires coordinated action across multiple fronts:

At the School Level

- **restoring hands-on learning programs** with modern equipment and industry-relevant curricula
- **creating career pathways** that connect middle school exploration to high school specialization to post-secondary training
- **partnering with local employers** to provide real-world experience and job placement opportunities
- **training counselors** to understand and promote trades careers alongside college options

At the Family Level

- **education campaigns** that inform parents about modern trades careers and earnings potential
- **family engagement programs** that include parents in career exploration activities
- **success story-sharing** that highlights diverse paths to middle-class prosperity

- **financial literacy education** that compares the total cost and return on investment of different post-secondary options

At the Policy Level

- **reauthorizing and expanding Perkins funding** to meet the scale of workforce needs

- **creating parity in guidance counseling** that gives equal attention to college and career paths

- **developing apprenticeship tax credits** that incentivize employer participation in training programs

- **measuring and rewarding schools** for career readiness outcomes, not just college enrollment rates

The Rising Tide

The good news is that change is already happening. Trade school enrollment is growing, employers are investing more in worker training, and young people are increasingly open to alternatives to traditional colleges.

Recent Trends

- Trade school enrollment grew from *9.6 million in 1999 to 16 million in 2014* (National Center for Education Statistics, 2015).

- Federal CTE funding reached *$1.4 billion in FY 2024*, up from previous years (*Estimated FY 2024 State Allocations*, 2024).

- Employer investment in worker training and apprenticeships is at historic highs.

- Multiple states have launched high-profile initiatives to promote skilled trades careers.

Industry Response

Companies are stepping up with innovative recruitment and training programs:

- paid apprenticeships that provide full-time wages during training

- partnership programs with high schools that create direct pathways to employment

- investment in modern training facilities and equipment

- mentorship programs that pair experienced workers with newcomers

It Takes All of Us

Teachers. Parents. Counselors. Politicians. Tradespeople. Veterans. Business owners. Union representatives. Mentors. Employers. Community leaders.

Everyone has a part to play in fixing the pipeline because this isn't just a labor shortage; it's a *values gap*. We've forgotten how to talk about work that isn't white-collar, and now, we're paying the price in unfilled jobs, crumbling infrastructure, and young people struggling with debt from degrees that don't lead to careers.

Specific Roles

- Teachers and counselors: Learn about modern trades careers and present them as viable first options, not fallback plans.

- Parents: Examine your own biases about what constitutes *success* and support your children's interests and aptitudes even if they don't align with traditional expectations.

- Employers–business owners: Invest in training programs, partner with schools, and create pathways for advancement that make trades careers attractive to ambitious young people.

- Policymakers: Fund career and technical education at levels that match workforce needs and remove barriers that artificially limit options for young people.

- Community leaders: Promote the value of skilled work and create local initiatives that connect young people with trades opportunities.

- Tradespeople: Share your stories, mentor newcomers, and serve as positive ambassadors for careers in the skilled trades.

The Vision of Success

Imagine a world where:

- High school students explore multiple pathways and make informed decisions based on their interests and aptitudes.

- Parents see a child choosing an apprenticeship with the same pride they'd feel about college acceptance.

- Guidance counselors have comprehensive knowledge about trades careers and present them enthusiastically.

- Employers work closely with schools to create seamless transitions from education to employment.

- Politicians measure success by workforce readiness and economic opportunity, not just test scores.

- Communities celebrate the skilled workers who build and maintain their infrastructure.

This isn't a utopian fantasy; it's an achievable goal that requires commitment, coordination, and a willingness to challenge outdated assumptions about education and careers.

But It's Fixable. If We Choose to Fix It

The pipeline problem didn't happen overnight and won't be solved overnight. But it can be solved. The solutions exist; we just need the will to implement them.

Every student who discovers a passion for skilled work, every parent who supports a nontraditional career path, every school that restores hands-on learning, every employer who invests in training, and every policymaker who prioritizes workforce needs over academic metrics contributes to fixing the pipeline.

The foundation is already there, built with the skills, knowledge, and dedication of generations of skilled workers. We just need to show young people where to find it and how to build on it.

We don't need to invent a new path for success; we just need to stop ignoring the one that's already built—with steel, sweat, and skilled hands.

Chapter 9:

Tool Belt Meets Tech—AI, Innovation, and the Future of the Trades

The trades may be rooted in tradition, but they're not stuck in the past.

In every corner of the skilled workforce—welding, electrical, HVAC, heavy equipment—you'll find new tools, smarter systems, and yes, even artificial intelligence. This chapter looks forward: how technology is shaping the trades, and why we need skilled people more than ever.

But first, let's address the elephant in the room: the fear that robots and AI will replace human workers. The reality is far more nuanced—and far more promising—than the headlines suggest.

The Evolution of Tools

It wasn't that long ago that blueprints were rolled out by hand and calculations done with pencil and paper. Today? Drones survey sites. Augmented reality previews a build. Digital modeling replaces guesswork. AI-powered estimating software can count objects across 5 pages of plans in less than 30 seconds per page (Barrett, 2024).

But none of these advances replace the *tradesperson*—they *empower* them. The teenager who is on the computer or gaming every day can also use those skills in the trades. There is hope for the computer geek out there.

The Internet of Things (IoT) on the Jobsite

You might not hear about it in the break room, but the Internet of Things (IoT) is already changing the trades.

IoT refers to "tools, gear, and equipment that are connected"—able to send and receive data in real time. It's not science fiction; it's sensors in your hard hat that detect fatigue. Boots that alert when you're standing too close to a hazard. Gas monitors that ping your phone when levels spike.

On construction sites and in industrial settings, IoT can:

- track environmental risks like heat, gas, or noise
- send automatic alerts when equipment is due for service
- help locate workers instantly in an emergency
- monitor safety compliance without someone watching over your shoulder

This isn't about replacing the trades; it's about protecting them. IoT helps keep workers alive, tools maintained, and jobsites smarter. And the future *tradesperson* will need to understand how to work with this tech, not as a programmer, but as a pro who knows how to use the tool correctly.

Modern Construction Technology

Building Information Modeling (BIM)

3D model-based processes that give architecture, engineering, and construction professionals tools to plan, design, construct, and manage buildings more efficiently. When combined with robotics, BIM data allows precise execution of complex tasks.

Autonomous Equipment

Self-driving bulldozers, excavators, and haul trucks equipped with GPS, LiDAR, and AI-powered navigation. These machines can perform complex operations with minimal human intervention while improving safety and precision.

Advanced Robotics

- Bricklaying robots like the Semiautomated Mason (SAM) can lay up to 3,000 bricks per day (Arabi, 2023).

- 3D printing robots construct entire building components layer by layer.

- Demolition robots operate remotely in hazardous environments.

- Robotic excavators and automated rebar-tying systems are transforming construction.

Smart Tools and IoT

- Laser-guided systems make cuts cleaner.

- AI-powered diagnostics speed up troubleshooting.

- Smart tools track usage and predict wear, preventing breakdowns before they happen.

Augmented and Virtual Reality

AR overlays digital information onto real-world construction sites, while VR allows virtual walk-throughs of projects before they're built.

That's not science fiction; it's the modern jobsite. And with all that innovation comes a growing need for workers who can bridge both worlds: practical skill *and* digital fluency.

The Reality of Automation in Construction

While headlines often proclaim that robots are coming to take construction jobs, the reality is far more complex. A recent study by the Midwest Economic Policy Institute estimates that by 2057, robots could potentially displace 2.7 million construction jobs. However, this projection assumes current automation trends continue linearly for 40 years, which rarely happens in practice (Manzo et al., 2018).

Current State of Construction Robotics

The global construction robot market was valued at *$420 million in 2021* and is projected to reach *$765 million by 2026* (Talpur, 2025). However, experts emphasize that this *robot revolution* is still in its infancy, and current robots are limited to simple, repetitive tasks.

What Robots Can Do Now

- lay bricks in controlled environments under human supervision
- perform basic demolition in hazardous areas
- execute simple excavation tasks on prepared sites
- apply paint or finish work in structured settings

What They Can't Do

- navigate complex, ever-changing jobsites independently

- make real-time decisions based on unexpected conditions
- perform the creative problem-solving that construction demands
- handle the full complexity of installation, maintenance, and repair work

As one industry expert noted, "A 2-year-old kid understands much more than a humanoid robot that is on the market today" (MIT Technology Review, 2023). The inherent complexity of construction work far exceeds what current automation can handle.

Maintenance Never Goes Out of Style

Here's the truth tech giants won't tell you: Even the smartest systems need humans to install, service, and repair them. Just as with all the AI buzz, if servers or other hardware and software fail in some way, humans still need to repair them.

Buildings don't maintain themselves. Pipes still leak. Circuits still blow. Roads still need patching. HVAC still needs seasonal tuning. That's not going away. Preventive or facilities maintenance is still going to be needed long into the future, and depending on what new technologies arise between now and then, humans are still going to be needed to upgrade to the new technology.

The more we build, the more maintenance we need. And the more complex the systems get, the more skilled the workers must be. The future isn't tech *instead of* trades; it's tech *within* the trades.

The Maintenance Reality

- The infrastructure continues to age and requires human expertise to maintain.

- New technologies create new systems that need specialized maintenance.

- Complex problems require human judgment and creative solutions.

- Emergency repairs can't wait for robot deployment and setup.

Jobs at Risk vs. Jobs Enhanced

Rather than wholesale replacement, most experts predict a transformation of roles within the trades. Research indicates that *47% of construction tasks* have automation potential (Manyika et al., 2017), but this doesn't mean 47% of jobs will disappear; it means those jobs will evolve.

Higher Risk Positions

- some welding tasks—particularly repetitive, standard welds
- basic bricklaying in controlled environments
- simple demolition work
- basic excavation tasks
- routine inspection work

Lower Risk Positions

- construction managers—zero percent automation risk
- civil engineers—low automation risk

- electricians—complex problem-solving and installation
- plumbers—varied manual tasks and human interaction
- HVAC technicians—diagnostic and repair work
- equipment operators—human judgment and adaptability

Enhanced Positions

Many trades workers will find their jobs enhanced rather than threatened by technology. AI and robotics can handle repetitive tasks, allowing workers to focus on complex problem-solving, quality control, and creative aspects of their work.

Why Human Skills Remain Essential

Construction involves qualities that current AI and robotics simply cannot replicate:

Physical Dexterity and Adaptability

Construction sites are *unstructured environments* that change constantly. Workers must adapt to varying conditions, handle unexpected obstacles, and make split-second decisions about safety and execution.

Problem-Solving and Creativity

Every construction project is unique. When problems arise—and they always do—human workers provide the creativity and judgment needed to find solutions that weren't in the original plans.

Human Interaction

Construction is fundamentally collaborative. Workers must communicate with team members, coordinate with other trades, interact with clients, and maintain safety awareness for everyone on site.

Quality Judgment

Experienced tradespeople develop an intuitive understanding of their craft that goes beyond mechanical execution. They can sense when something isn't right, make quality judgments, and adjust their approach accordingly.

Contextual Understanding

Human workers understand the broader context of their work—how their task fits into the overall project, what the end user needs, and how to balance competing priorities.

Reality Check: Robots Don't Replace Pride

You can't automate integrity.

You can't code the gut feeling that tells you something's off in a weld. You can't digitize the mentorship that happens on a scaffold. You can't replace the human judgment it takes to do hard things safely.

AI might help you measure faster, but it won't climb the ladder for you.

Recent real-world experience confirms this. Construction companies that have experimented with robots often find that the machines require more human oversight than anticipated. One construction manager, Hector Guerra (2022) described trying a bricklaying robot touted for 24-7 operation:

> "The machine couldn't work on its own. It still needed people to operate it: one feeding it bricks, the other mortar on the other side. Then, when the machine was done in its current location, it had to be moved to a new spot and set up all over again... The machine wound up costing more to operate than skilled labor" (Guerra, 2022).

That's where pride still lives: in the doing, in the fixing, and in the hands-on, boots-on-the-ground, real-world experience that no AI, app, or robot can replicate.

The Collaborative Future

Rather than replacement, the future points toward collaboration between humans and machines. This *human-robot collaborative construction* model leverages the strengths of both.

Robots excel at:

- repetitive, precise tasks
- working in hazardous environments
- consistent output over long periods
- handling heavy materials
- following predetermined patterns

Humans excel at:

- complex problem-solving
- adapting to changing conditions

- quality assessment and judgment
- safety awareness and decision-making
- communication and coordination
- creative solutions to unique challenges

Examples of Successful Collaboration

- Robots handle the physical lifting and placement in bricklaying while masons oversee quality and handle complex patterns.
- Automated equipment performs basic excavation while operators manage precision work and safety oversight.
- AI assists with project planning and scheduling while project managers handle client relations and problem-solving.
- Smart tools provide data and diagnostics while technicians interpret results and make repair decisions.

New Opportunities in Tech-Enhanced Trades

Technology isn't just changing existing jobs; it's creating entirely new career opportunities within the trades:

- Robotics technicians: Workers who install, maintain, and repair construction robots. This field combines traditional mechanical skills with programming and troubleshooting abilities.
- AI equipment specialists: Professionals who calibrate, operate, and maintain AI-powered construction tools and systems.

- Digital construction coordinators: Workers who manage the interface between digital systems—BIM, project management software, IoT sensors—and physical construction work.

- Automation safety specialists: Experts who ensure safe interaction between human workers and automated systems on construction sites.

- Predictive maintenance technicians: Workers who use AI-powered diagnostic tools to predict and prevent equipment failures before they occur.

Upskilling for the Future

The construction industry is actively investing in worker education to bridge the technology gap:

- Industry training programs: Trade schools are incorporating AI and robotics into their curricula, teaching students to work alongside advanced technology.

- Government support: Canadian and U.S. government programs provide subsidies for workers to afford upskilling courses in technology-related construction skills (U.S. Department of Labor, 2024).

- Employer investment: Companies are providing on-the-job training in new technologies, recognizing that their experienced workers bring irreplaceable knowledge that needs to be combined with technical skills.

- Continuous learning: The most successful tradespeople of the future will be those who embrace lifelong learning, adapting to new tools and techniques throughout their careers.

Embracing What's Next—Without Losing What Matters

We don't need to fear change, but we do need to guide it.

Tech can improve safety by identifying hazards before they cause accidents. It can speed up jobs by automating time-consuming tasks. It can open doors to people who once felt locked out of the industry by making physically demanding work more accessible.

But only if we ensure that the people driving those tools still know the craft underneath. Technology should enhance human capability, not replace human judgment.

This means:

- **Training programs that include both tools *and* tech:** Modern apprenticeships must teach traditional skills alongside digital fluency.

- **Outreach that shows trades as modern and forward-facing:** Recruiting efforts should highlight the high-tech aspects of modern construction to attract digitally native young people.

- **Leadership that welcomes innovation without replacing identity:** Industry leaders must embrace technological advancement while preserving the pride, craftsmanship, and human connections that define skilled trades.

The best tradespeople of tomorrow will still be problem-solvers, teammates, and masters of their environment. They'll just have better gear—and the skills to use it effectively.

The Labor Shortage Solution

The current adoption of technology is largely driven by necessity rather than choice. An AGC workforce survey shows that "88% of construction firms are having difficulty finding workers to hire (2023 Workforce Survey, 2023)." The combination of veteran workers nearing retirement and insufficient numbers of new skilled workers entering the field has created a crisis that technology helps address.

Rather than replacing workers, current automation focuses on:

- **augmenting the productivity** of existing workers
- **reducing physical strain** to help workers stay in the field longer
- **improving safety** to prevent injuries that remove workers from the workforce
- **attracting new workers** who are comfortable with technology

This approach considers technology a tool to support and enhance human workers rather than eliminate them.

Global Perspectives on Automation

International experience provides insight into the future of construction automation:

- **Canada:** Government and industry programs focus on upskilling workers to work alongside AI and automation, recognizing that hybrid roles combining traditional expertise with technological knowledge are the future (Construction Association of Canada, 2024).

- **Advanced economies:** IMF research indicates that while 60% of jobs in advanced economies are exposed to AI, most construction workers will find the technology complementary rather than disruptive (Cazzaniga et al., 2024).

- **Manufacturing comparison:** In manufacturing, where automation is much more advanced (79% adoption vs. 55% in construction), robots have largely enhanced rather than replaced human workers, creating new job categories and increasing productivity (World Economic Forum, 2025).

Environmental and Efficiency Benefits

Technology integration also serves broader social goals:

- **Sustainability:** Robots optimize material use and reduce waste. For instance, 3D printing allows for precise, eco-friendly construction with lower carbon footprints.

- **Efficiency:** Automated systems work continuously without fatigue, accelerating project timelines and reducing costs.

- **Safety:** Remote-operated equipment reduces human exposure to dangerous conditions, while AI systems can predict and prevent accidents.

- **Quality:** Consistent robotic precision reduces errors and rework, creating better final products.

The Human Element That Can't Be Coded

Despite all technological advances, certain aspects of construction work remain fundamentally human:

- **Craftsmanship:** The pride and attention to detail that separate good work from great work cannot be programmed.

- **Mentorship:** The knowledge transfer from experienced workers to newcomers happens through human relationships and cannot be automated.

- **Community:** Construction work builds not just structures but communities of workers who support each other through challenges.

- **Adaptability:** The ability to improvise, solve unexpected problems, and adapt to changing conditions remains uniquely human.

- **Purpose:** The satisfaction of building something meaningful, contributing to community infrastructure, and seeing tangible results of your work speaks to fundamental human needs that technology cannot fulfill.

Looking Forward

The future of the trades will be defined not by choosing between humans and machines but by how effectively we integrate both. The most successful construction companies will be those that do the following:

- invest in worker training and development

- adopt technology thoughtfully to enhance rather than replace human capabilities

- maintain focus on quality, safety, and craftsmanship

- create pathways for workers to grow with technological change

- preserve the human relationships and pride that make skilled work meaningful

Young people entering the trades today will work with tools their predecessors couldn't imagine, but the fundamental values of skilled work—precision, reliability, teamwork, and pride in accomplishment—will remain unchanged.

The world will keep changing, but it will always need someone to build it, fix it, and keep it running. Technology will make us better at that work, but it will never replace the human heart that drives it.

Chapter 10:
Rebuilding Respect, One Trade at a Time

Respect isn't given. It's built—just like the bridges, the buildings, and the backbone of this country.

This final chapter is about what it means to bring that respect back: for the work, for the workers, and for the future we're still building. After nine chapters of examining where we've been and where we're going, it's time to talk about the most important question of all:

How do we rebuild the honor that skilled work deserves?

Why Respect Matters: More Than You Think

When people don't respect your work, they undervalue your life. They ignore your safety, they cut your training, they treat your career like a consolation prize. But the impact goes deeper than individual dignity; it affects entire communities, economies, and the future of American infrastructure.

The Real Cost of Disrespect

Consider what happens when society devalues skilled trades:

- **Infrastructure decay:** The American Society of Civil Engineers gives U.S. infrastructure a C- grade, estimating a $2.6 trillion investment gap by 2029 (American Society of Civil Engineers, 2021).

- **Skills shortage crisis:** The construction industry needs approximately 723,000 workers per year (Labor Report Shows Dire Need, 2024).

- **Economic inefficiency:** Projects take longer, cost more, and often fail when we don't have enough skilled workers or when corners are cut on training and safety.

- **Generational knowledge loss:** When experienced tradespeople retire without proper succession, decades of accumulated wisdom disappear.

But when respect *is* present? You feel it in the handshake, the contract, and the way a kid looks up to you and says, "I want to do what you do." You see it in the budgets allocated for safety equipment, the time given for proper training, and the recognition that skilled work requires both intelligence and experience.

The Multiplier Effect of Respect

Research from the Georgetown Center on Education and the Workforce shows that when skilled trades are valued and properly supported (Camevale et al., 2021):

- Worker productivity increases by 25–40%.

- Job satisfaction scores rival or exceed those of college-educated professionals.

- Safety incidents decrease by up to 60% when workers feel valued and properly trained.

- Communities see stronger economic development and infrastructure resilience.

Rebuilding that respect means reminding the world that we don't just build things; we build *nations*. Every time the lights stay on, the roads hold firm, the plumbing works, and the structure stands, we're proving that this work matters.

Work That Leaves a Mark: The Legacy Advantage

There's a reason tradespeople take their families on drives to show them what they built.

"That bridge? I tied the rebar in that." "That building? I welded the beams." "That power grid? I ran those lines."

It's not bragging; it's a legacy. And legacy is something college debt doesn't buy.

The Tangible Impact Difference

While knowledge workers often struggle to point to concrete results of their labor, skilled tradespeople create visible, lasting contributions to society:

- Generational impact: The Golden Gate Bridge, built by skilled workers in the 1930s, still carries 112,000 vehicles daily—nearly 90 years later (12 Golden Gate Bridge Fun Facts, n.d.).

- Community building: Every hospital, school, and fire station represents skilled trades workers who literally built the infrastructure that saves lives and serves communities.

- Economic foundation: Manufacturing facilities, power plants, and transportation networks—all requiring skilled trades—form the backbone of economic activity.

Modern Legacy Projects

Today's tradespeople are building tomorrow's landmarks:

- wind farms that will power communities for decades

- smart buildings with integrated technology systems
- high-speed rail networks and modern transit systems
- green infrastructure that addresses climate challenges
- advanced manufacturing facilities bringing production back to America

Tradespeople don't just leave behind pay stubs; they leave behind *proof*—in steel, concrete, wire, and pipe. That kind of work deserves honor, and we can restore it.

Reality Check: We Lost a Generation to Screens, but Recovery Is Possible

It's harsh, but it's true. We've lost a whole generation to video games, digital escapes, and the comfort of not trying.

Not everyone, of course, but enough. Enough that there's now a massive gap between what needs to be built and who is willing to build it.

The Numbers Tell the Story

- Screen time crisis: American teenagers spend over 7 hours daily on screens, with only 23% reporting regular physical activity (Rideout et al., 2021).
- Skills Gap: The majority of young adults cannot perform basic tasks like changing a tire, using basic tools, or understanding how their home's systems work.

- Disconnection from Physical Work: The share of high school students who have taken a shop class has declined sharply since 1980.

But There's Hope in the Data

Recent trends show encouraging signs of change:

- Maker movement growth: While physical maker spaces actually declined in number after 2020 due to pandemic restrictions, digital DIY culture experienced significant growth, with craft marketplaces and online maker communities seeing unprecedented engagement from young people rediscovering hands-on creation.

- Trade school enrollment: Community college programs in skilled trades have seen an enrollment increase over the past years.

- Social media influence: Platforms like TikTok and YouTube feature skilled tradespeople with millions of followers, showing young people that trades can be both modern and respected.

The Gaming Connection

Interestingly, multiple skills that make great gamers translate directly into modern trades:

- **Problem-solving under pressure:** Critical in construction and repair work.

- **Hand-eye coordination:** Essential for precision work.

- **Systems thinking:** Understanding how complex systems interact.

- **Continuous learning:** Modern trades require constant skill updates, just like gaming.

As we noted in Chapter 9, "The teenager who is on the computer or gaming every day can use those skills in the trades also. There is hope for the computer geek out there."

So, we start now. We rebuild one conversation at a time. One mentorship at a time. One shop class at a time.

We reintroduce *real work* to people who've never held a hammer—and remind them what it feels like to do something that matters.

The Economic Case for Respect

Beyond the moral argument for respecting skilled work lies a compelling economic reality: Countries and communities that honor their skilled trades consistently outperform those that don't.

International Examples

- Germany: Apprenticeship programs are so respected that over 50% of students choose vocational training over university (*The German Vocational Training System: An Overview*, n.d.).

- **Switzerland:** Median income for skilled trades exceeds the OECD average, and the country consistently ranks highly in global competitiveness.

- **South Korea:** After decades of university-focused culture, they're now investing in vocational education because they recognize that the skilled worker shortage threatens their economic future.

The American Opportunity

If we rebuild respect for skilled trades in America, the economic benefits would be substantial:

- GDP impact: The construction industry, which contributes $1.2 trillion (4.5% of GDP) to the U.S. economy, faces a shortage of nearly 500,000 workers, resulting in billions in annual economic losses from project delays (*GDP by Industry*, 2025).

- Infrastructure efficiency: Properly trained, respected workers complete projects faster with fewer safety incidents.

- Innovation catalyst: When skilled workers are valued, they drive innovation from the ground up—the people doing the work often know best how to improve it.

Breaking Down the Barriers: Systemic Changes Needed

Rebuilding respect requires more than individual attitude changes: We need systemic shifts in how society views, structures, and supports skilled work.

Educational Reform

The current education system actively discourages skilled trades by treating them as *backup plans*. What we need is:

- Career pathway equality: Presenting skilled trades as first-choice careers, not consolation prizes.

- Guidance counselor training: Most high school counselors know little about modern trades and their earning potential.

- Hands-on learning: Reintroducing shop classes, technical education, and maker spaces to all schools.

- Parent education: Helping parents understand that skilled trades offer secure, well-paying careers.

Media Representation

Popular culture shapes perceptions, and skilled trades have been poorly represented:

- Current reality: TV shows and movies often portray tradespeople as uneducated, crude, or unsuccessful.

- Needed change: Showcasing skilled trades professionals as problem-solvers, innovators, and essential community members.

- Success stories: Highlighting tradespeople who've built successful businesses, contributed to major projects, or developed innovative solutions.

Workplace Culture

Within the trades themselves, culture must evolve to welcome and respect all workers:

- Inclusive environment: Creating welcoming spaces for women, minorities, and people from all backgrounds.

- Mentorship programs: Formalizing knowledge transfer from experienced workers to newcomers.

- Continuous learning: Supporting ongoing education and skill development.

- Safety culture: Prioritizing worker safety as a demonstration of respect and value.

The Demographic Revolution: New Faces, Same Values

The face of skilled trades is changing, and that is a cause for optimism, not concern.

Women in the Trades

- Women now represent 11% of construction workers(McGriff, 2025; Women in the Labor Force, 2023).

- In electrical work, women earn nearly as much as men earn—one of the smallest gender pay gaps in any field.

- Diverse firms' productivity is 1.32 times higher than that of firms lacking diversity, according to research examining U.S.-based computer companies and Fortune 500 firms (Richard et al., 2021).

Military Veterans

- Veterans bring discipline, technical training, and leadership skills to civilian trades.

- According to the U.S. Bureau of Labor Statistics, the share of employed veterans working in the construction industry increased to 6.5% in 2022 (*Employment Situation*, 2023).

- Some veteran-owned construction companies rank among the top-rated contractors in their regions.

Second-Career Professionals

- Data shows that under-19s only account for 23% of apprenticeship starts, meaning 77% are 19 or older (Career Change, 2025).

- Career changers often become highly effective because they chose trades deliberately rather than defaulting to them.

- Many bring business, communication, or technical skills from previous careers.

The Common Thread

Despite changing demographics, successful tradespeople share core characteristics:

- pride in quality work
- commitment to continuous learning
- strong problem-solving skills
- reliability and integrity
- understanding that their work serves something larger than themselves

Technology as a Respect Builder

As explored in Chapter 9, technology isn't threatening skilled trades; it's elevating them. This technological evolution is helping rebuild respect by doing the following:

Attracting Digital Natives

- Modern construction uses drones, 3D modeling, and AI-powered tools.
- Young people see trades as high-tech, innovative fields rather than outdated industries.
- Virtual and augmented reality training makes learning more engaging and effective.

Improving Working Conditions

- Robotic assistance reduces physical strain and injury risk.
- Smart tools provide real-time feedback and prevent errors.
- Better safety monitoring protects workers and demonstrates employer respect.

Enhancing Problem-Solving

- access to technical databases and troubleshooting apps
- real-time communication with experts and colleagues
- predictive maintenance technology that prevents problems before they occur

Creating New Career Paths

- robotics technicians for construction equipment
- digital system specialists
- AI-assisted project coordinators

- smart building maintenance experts

- safety professionals with the insider knowledge of how the trades work

The key insight from Chapter 9 remains: "Technology should enhance human capability, not replace human judgment."

The Road Back Is Built Together—A Comprehensive Strategy

No single policy will fix this. No single school. No single parent. But together? We can rebuild the reputation of the trades until there's pride in every path—not just the academic ones.

Individual Actions That Matter

Speaking Proudly About Trade Careers

- Share success stories of skilled tradespeople.
- Correct misconceptions when you hear them.
- Highlight the skill, intelligence, and problem-solving required.
- Emphasize earning potential and job security.

Supporting Hands-on Programs and Training

- Vote for school board candidates who support technical education.
- Donate tools or time to local trade programs.

- Mentor young people interested in skilled work.
- Support apprenticeship programs through taxes and advocacy.

Calling Out Disrespect When We See It

- Challenge stereotypes in media and conversation.
- Demand proper safety equipment and training from employers.
- Report wage theft and workplace violations.
- Stand up for colleagues facing discrimination.

Setting the Example for the Next Generation

- Demonstrate professionalism and expertise in your work.
- Continue learning and adapting to new technologies.
- Share knowledge generously with newcomers.
- Take pride in your contribution to society.

Community-Level Changes

School Districts

- reinstating shop classes and technical education programs
- creating partnerships with local employers for internships and apprenticeships
- ensuring guidance counselors understand trade career paths
- showcasing successful local tradespeople as role models

Local Governments

- enforcing prevailing wage laws that ensure fair compensation
- supporting apprenticeship programs through public contracts
- investing in modern equipment for public technical schools
- creating pathways from military service to civilian trades careers

Employers

- offering competitive wages and comprehensive benefits
- providing ongoing training and career development opportunities
- creating safe, respectful work environments
- investing in modern tools and technology

Industry-Wide Initiatives

Professional Organizations

- developing certification programs that demonstrate expertise
- creating continuing education requirements that ensure quality
- advocating for fair wages and working conditions
- promoting the industry through public relations efforts

Union and Nonunion Cooperation

- working together on training standards and safety protocols

- jointly advocating for infrastructure investment
- sharing best practices for recruitment and retention
- presenting a united front on industry issues

Measuring Success: What Victory Looks Like

How will we know when we've successfully rebuilt respect for skilled trades? Here are the concrete indicators to watch for:

Economic Indicators

- wage growth in skilled trades keeping pace with or exceeding inflation
- decreased vacancy rates in skilled positions
- increased investment in training and apprenticeship programs
- a growing number of worker-owned cooperatives and small businesses

Social Indicators

- increased enrollment in technical education programs
- more positive media representation of skilled work
- parents encouraging children to consider trade careers
- politicians and community leaders highlighting trades in economic development plans

Workplace Indicators

- improved safety records across all trades
- decreased turnover and increased job satisfaction
- more diverse workforce reflecting community demographics
- innovation and technological adoption driven by worker input

Cultural Indicators

- young people expressing interest in hands-on careers
- social media celebrating skilled work and craftsmanship
- community recognition of local tradespeople and their contributions
- integration of skilled trades into broader definitions of professional success

The Generational Bridge: Learning From Each Other

One of the most promising aspects of rebuilding respect is the opportunity to bridge generational differences within the trades.

What Experienced Workers Bring

- deep knowledge of materials, techniques, and problem-solving approaches

- understanding safety practices developed through years of experience
- client relationship skills and business knowledge
- mentorship and training abilities

What Younger Workers Bring

- comfort with new technologies and digital tools
- fresh perspectives on efficiency and problem-solving
- diverse backgrounds and experiences
- energy and enthusiasm for innovation

Creating Successful Partnerships

- formal mentorship programs that pair experienced workers with newcomers
- cross-training initiatives where older workers learn technology while teaching traditional skills
- project teams that intentionally mix generations and experience levels
- recognition programs that celebrate both innovation and traditional craftsmanship

Global Competition and National Security

Rebuilding respect for skilled trades isn't just about individual careers; it's about national competitiveness and security.

The Strategic Reality

Countries that maintain strong, skilled workforces have significant advantages:

- Manufacturing capability: Essential for both economic growth and national defense.

- Infrastructure resilience: Critical for withstanding natural disasters and maintaining supply chains.

- Innovation capacity: Skilled workers often drive practical innovations that improve efficiency and quality.

- Economic independence: Reduced reliance on foreign labor and imports.

Current Challenges

The US faces serious disadvantages due to the skilled worker shortage:

- Reshoring difficulties: Companies wanting to bring manufacturing back to America struggle to find qualified workers.

- Infrastructure vulnerability: Aging systems require skilled maintenance that we may not have the capacity to provide.

- Innovation lag: Other countries are advancing faster in areas requiring skilled implementation of new technologies.

The Path Forward

Rebuilding respect for skilled trades is ultimately about rebuilding American capacity to create, maintain, and innovate in the physical world.

This requires:

- sustained investment in education and training
- cultural change that values all forms of productive work
- policy support for apprenticeships and career development
- recognition that skilled work is essential to national strength

Beyond Individual Success: Building Community

The ultimate goal of rebuilding respect goes beyond individual career success; it's about rebuilding communities where all productive work is valued, where people take pride in contributing to something larger than themselves, and where young people see multiple pathways to meaningful, prosperous lives.

What Healthy Trade Communities Look Like

- Economic diversity: Multiple career paths providing good living for families.
- Intergenerational connection: Older workers passing knowledge to younger ones while learning from them.
- Civic engagement: Skilled workers involved in community leadership and decision-making.
- Innovation culture: Continuous improvement and adaptation while maintaining quality standards.
- Inclusive environment: Welcoming to all people regardless of background, gender, or ethnicity.

The Ripple Effects

When communities respect and support skilled trades:

- Local economies become more resilient and diverse.

- Young people have more options for building successful lives.

- Infrastructure is better maintained and more reliable.

- Innovation increases as practical knowledge combines with new technologies.

- Social cohesion strengthens as people see the value in different types of contributions.

A Personal Challenge: What Will You Do?

This book isn't just a story; it's a start. But it's only the beginning if readers take action.

To Current Tradespeople

- Mentor someone new to the field.

- Continue learning and adapting to new technologies.

- Speak proudly about your work and its importance.

- Demand respect through excellent performance and professionalism.

- Support policies and candidates who value skilled work.

To Parents and Educators

- Learn about modern trade careers and their opportunities.
- Encourage young people to explore hands-on work.
- Support technical education programs in your community.
- Challenge your own biases about what constitutes success.
- Recognize that college isn't the only path to a good life.

To Business and Community Leaders

- Invest in training and development for skilled workers.
- Pay fair wages and provide good working conditions.
- Speak publicly about the importance of skilled trades.
- Support policies that strengthen technical education.
- Partner with schools and training programs.

To Young People

- Explore opportunities in skilled trades with an open mind.
- Understand that these careers offer both security and growth potential.
- Don't let others' biases limit your choices.
- Consider how your interests and strengths might translate to skilled work.
- Remember that meaningful work comes in many forms.

The Long View: Building for Generations

Rebuilding respect for skilled trades is a generational project. It won't happen overnight, but every action counts, every conversation matters, and every young person who discovers a passion for skilled work makes a difference.

What Success Will Look Like in 20 Years

Imagine an America where:

- High school students compete as eagerly for apprenticeships as for college admissions.

- Skilled tradespeople are recognized as essential professionals deserving of respect and fair compensation.

- Communities celebrate both their doctors and electricians, their lawyers and plumbers.

- Innovation flows from the combination of traditional craftsmanship and cutting-edge technology.

- Infrastructure is maintained by proud, skilled workers using the best tools and techniques available.

The Foundation We're Building

Every beam raised, every student trained, and every hand offered to lift someone up—it all counts. It all builds toward a future where:

- Work is valued based on its contribution to society, not just its educational requirements.

- Young people have multiple pathways to prosperity and fulfillment.

- Communities are economically resilient because they value all forms of productive work.

- America maintains the skilled workforce necessary for economic competitiveness and national security.

Conclusion:
The Choice Before Us

We stand at a crossroads.

We can continue down the path of devaluing skilled work, watching our infrastructure decay and our communities lose economic diversity, or we can choose to rebuild respect, one trade at a time, one worker at a time, one community at a time.

The choice isn't just about careers; it's about what kind of society we want to be. Do we want a society that values only certain types of intelligence and success? Or do we want one that recognizes and rewards all the different ways people contribute to our collective prosperity and security?

To the builders, the welders, the pipe fitters, the riggers, the laborers, the apprentices, the veterans, the women, the mentors, the journeymen, the ones who never gave up—*this is for you.*

Your work matters. Your knowledge matters. Your contribution to society matters.

And to everyone else: The future we build depends not just on the skill of our hands but on the respect we show for the work that literally builds our world.

Respect doesn't come back all at once. And in the end, respect—like everything else worth having—is something we build together.

Epilogue:
For the Ones Who Showed Up

Some never understood why we chose this life. The early mornings. The busted knuckles. The sweat in winter. The sunburns in summer.

But we know why.

We chose it because there's something sacred about building something real. Something heavy. Something permanent. We chose it because our names may not be on plaques, but our work *stands*—in concrete, in steel, in legacy.

This book isn't just a rally cry for the next generation; it's a thank you to the ones who came before. To those who taught us to tie off right. To cut clean. To keep our heads on a swivel and our pride in our craft.

Some of them didn't make it home, and yet their work lives on—inside the welds, the wire, the form, and the finish. They gave their strength to something bigger than themselves. And we remember them.

We walk past memorials of their work every day and don't even realize it.

But we do. We remember.

The Shift Is Coming

Something is changing out there. I see it in the young faces showing up at apprenticeship programs. I hear it in the conversations between parents who are starting to understand that college isn't the only path to a good life. I feel it in the respect that's slowly being rebuilt, one project at a time.

The tool belt generation is coming. They're choosing apprenticeships over debt. They're seeing through the college-for-all myth. They're discovering what we've always known: that working with your hands isn't settling for less. It's choosing something real.

But they need us. They need our knowledge, our stories, our willingness to teach. They need to understand that this work isn't just about paychecks; it's about legacy, honor, and the deep satisfaction of building something that serves others.

The Promise We Make

Let this also be a promise: To the next generation, we won't let your work be invisible.

We'll teach you what we know. We'll show you what it means to stand in boots that have earned their wear. We'll keep the stories alive—because those stories matter.

We'll show you how to work safely, because every worker deserves to go home. We'll teach you the tribal knowledge that isn't written down anywhere—the tricks, the shortcuts, and the wisdom earned through years of getting it right.

We'll help you understand that technology doesn't threaten what we do; it makes us better at it.

The future belongs to people who can think and build, who can solve problems with both their minds and hands.

And to those who think this is just work?

It's more than that.

It's honor. It's memory. Its purpose. It's *ours*.

The Work Continues

The conversation doesn't end with this book. It continues every time someone chooses an apprenticeship. Every time a parent supports their child's passion for skilled work. Every time a worker mentors a newcomer. Every time someone challenges the old assumptions about what success looks like.

We're building more than structures. We're building respect. We're building opportunity. We're building a future where all honest work is valued, young people have real choices, and communities understand that their prosperity depends on the skilled hands that build and maintain everything they rely on.

The foundation is solid. Now, let's keep building on it.

We don't stop when the shift ends; we stop when the job is done. And the job is never just about the work; it's about who we do it for.

Resources

Trade Union Resources

If you're interested in learning more about apprenticeship opportunities and career paths in skilled trades, these national trade union websites provide comprehensive information about training programs, local unions, and career opportunities:

Building Trades Unions

International Brotherhood of Boilermakers (IBB) *https://www.boilermakers.org*

Boilermakers work in heavy industry construction, shipbuilding, railroads, cement, mining, and related industries.

United Brotherhood of Carpenters and Joiners of America (UBC) **https://www.carpenters.org**

Carpenters work in residential and commercial construction, including framing, finish work, and specialty carpentry.

International Brotherhood of Electrical Workers (IBEW) *https://www.ibew.org*

Electricians work in construction, utilities, telecommunications, broadcasting, manufacturing, and government.

International Association of Bridge, Structural, Ornamental and Reinforcing Iron Workers
https://www.ironworkers.org

Ironworkers erect structural steel and iron for bridges, buildings, and other structures.

Laborers' International Union of North America (LIUNA) https://www.liuna.org

Laborers work in construction, environmental remediation, and general construction support.

United Association of Journeymen and Apprentices of the Plumbing and Pipe Fitting Industry (UA)
https://www.ua.org

Pipe fitters, plumbers, steamfitters, and welders work in the construction and service of piping systems.

International Union of Operating Engineers (IUOE)
https://www.iuoe.org

Operating engineers operate cranes, bulldozers, and other heavy equipment in construction.

Sheet Metal Workers' International Association (SMWIA) https://www.smwia.org

Sheet metal workers fabricate and install heating, ventilation, and air conditioning systems.

International Union of Painters and Allied Trades (IUPAT) https://www.iupat.org

Painters and allied trades workers handle finish work, including painting, drywall, and glazing.

United Union of Roofers, Waterproofers and Allied Workers https://www.unionroofers.com

Roofers install and repair roofing systems on residential and commercial buildings.

Additional Resources

Building Trades Unions–North America's Building Trades Unions) https://www.buildingtradeunions.org

Umbrella organization representing building trades unions across North America.

Helmets to Hardhats
https://www.helmetstohardhats.org

Helps military service members transition to careers in the construction industry.

National Center for Construction Education and Research (NCCER) https://www.nccer.org

Develops standardized curriculum and assessments for construction craft training.

U.S. Department of Labor–Office of Apprenticeship
https://www.apprenticeship.gov

Federal resource for apprenticeship programs and career information.

Women Build Nations
https://www.womenbuildnations.org

Supports women entering and advancing in construction careers.

National Association of Women in Construction (NAWIC)
https://www.nawic.org

Professional association for women in construction-related careers.

Many of these unions have local chapters throughout the United States and Canada. Contact information for local unions can be found on the respective national websites. Most offer apprenticeship programs that combine paid on-the-job training with classroom instruction, leading to journey-level certification and lifelong career opportunities.

About the Author

K. A. Pierce has spent over 3 decades living the lessons found in this book. With 14 years of experience as a carpenter and ironworker—and nearly 2 decades as a safety professional—she brings grit, wisdom, and firsthand perspective to every page. One of only a few women in her Ironworkers Local, she knows what it means to build, to lead, and to prove you belong.

Her time in the trades shaped her approach to safety—not just as a job, but as a responsibility. Because she's climbed the steel, worked on the scaffolds, and faced the hazards, she brings credibility and care to every site she protects.

Today, she's a passionate advocate for trades education, mentorship, and the next generation of blue-collar workers.

Author's Note

This manuscript represents a comprehensive examination of the skilled trades in America, drawing from personal experience, extensive research, and interviews with workers across multiple industries. All statistics and citations have been verified to the best of our ability at the time of publication.

The stories and experiences shared throughout this book, while specific in their details, represent broader patterns and challenges faced by millions of skilled workers across the country.

Names and identifying details have been changed in some cases to protect privacy, but the essence of each story remains true to the experiences of those who shared them.

Special thanks to all the tradespeople who opened up about their experiences, challenges, and triumphs. Your stories are the foundation upon which this book stands.

All product names, logos, and brands are the property of their respective owners. YouTube, Instagram, TikTok, and LinkedIn are registered trademarks of their respective corporations.

Copyright © 2025 by K. A. Pierce

All rights reserved. No part of this book may be reproduced or used in any manner without the written permission of the copyright owner, except for the use of quotations in a book review.

First edition 2025

ISBN [to be assigned]

Published by KAJE Legacy LLC

Printed in the United States of America

References

AAA. (2023). *Young adults and basic automotive maintenance survey*. American Automobile Association.

American Society of Civil Engineers. (2021). *2021 infrastructure report card*.

Annual Report 2024. (2024). The National Association of Women in Construction. https://nawic.com.au/Common/Uploaded%20files/Smart%20Suite/Smart%20Library/124bcafc-029f-467c-8f53-0699c1128879/Nawic%20Annual%20Report%202024%20updated%2011%2008%202024.pdf

Apprenticeship continues to demonstrate strong growth. (2021). U.S. Department of Labor. https://www.dol.gov/agencies/eta/apprenticeship/about/statistics/2021#:~:text=In%20FY%202021%2C%20more%20than

Arabi, K. (2023). Construction robots in 2024: A comprehensive guide. *Neuroject*. https://neuroject.com/construction-robots/

Augmented reality for training your workforce. (2025). *Aidar*. https://aidarsolutions.com/augmented-reality-for-training/#:~:text=Augmented%20reality%20(AR)%20for%20training

Bailey, K. (2024). Mike Rowe reveals how he'd spend Trump's proposed $3B trade school windfall. *Fox Business*. https://www.foxbusiness.com/media/mike-rowe-reveals-spend-trumps-proposed-3b-trade-school-windfall

Barrett, K. (2024). A new world of construction with AI & robotics. *Construct Connect.* https://www.constructconnect.com/blog/construction-robotics

Camevale, A. P., Cheah, B., & Wenzinger, E. (2021). *The college payoff: More education doesn't always mean more earnings.* Georgetown University Center on Education and the Workforce.

Career change through apprenticeships: A guide for adults. (2025). *Total People.* https://www.totalpeople.co.uk/about/news-blogs/career-change-apprenticeship-for-adults/

Cazzaniga, M., Jaumotte, F., Li, L., Melina, G., Panton, A. J., Pizzinelli, C., Rockall, E. J., & Tavares, M. M. (2024). *Gen-AI: Artificial intelligence and the future of work.* Staff Discussion Notes. https://doi.org/10.5089/9798400262548.006International

Clark, P. (2025). *[2025 update] 44 construction safety statistics for 2025.* Claris. https://www.clarisdesignbuild.com/41-construction-safety-statistics/.

College Board Advocacy and Access Communities. (2023). *National Center for Education statistics report: Condition of education.* College Board. https://advocacycommunities.collegeboard.org/discussion/168/national-center-for-education-statistics-report-condition-of-education

College enrollment rates. (2024). National Center for Education Statistics. https://nces.ed.gov/programs/coe/indicator/cpb/college-enrollment-rate

Construction wage growth and labor market dynamics. (2024). McKinsey & Company.

Coshow, J. (2019). The death of shop class: The history and decline. *Dunn Lumber.* https://www.dunnlumber.com/blog/post/the-death-of-shop-class-history-and-decline

Crawford, M. B. (2009). *Shop class as soulcraft: An inquiry into the value of work.* Penguin Press.

The Demographic Outlook: 2024 to 2054. (2024). Congressional Budget Office. https://www.cbo.gov/publication/59899

The employment situation — May 2020. (2020). Bureau of Labor Statistics. https://www.bls.gov/news.release/archives/empsit_06052020.pdf

Employment situation of veterans news release. (2023). U.S. Bureau of Labor Statistics. https://www.bls.gov/news.release/archives/vet_03212023.htm

Estimated FY 2024 state allocations under the Carl D. Perkins Career and Technical Education Act. (2024). U.S. Department of Education, Office of Career, Technical, and Adult Education. https://cte.ed.gov/grants/state-formula-grants/state-allocations

Federal student loan portfolio. (n.d.). https://studentaid.gov/data-center/student/portf

Feuer, A. (2018, September 11). Death toll from 9/11-related illnesses will soon pass number killed on that day. *The New York Times.*

Fishman, R., Hiler, T., & Nguyen, S. (2021). One semester later: How prospective and current college students' perspectives of higher ed have changed between August and December 2020. *New America.* https://www.newamerica.org/education-policy/edcentral/higher-ed-tracking-survey/

47% of U.S. employees forced to self-train due to lack of knowledge transfer from retiring employees. (2022). Express. https://www.expresspros.com/newsroom/news-releases/news-releases/2022/05/47-of-u-s-employees-forced-to-self-train-due-to-lack-of-knowledge-transfer-from-retiring-employees

Freifeld, L. (2023). 2023 training industry report. *Training Magazine.* https://trainingmag.com/2023-training-industry-report/

Fry, R. (2020). *The pace of Boomer retirements has accelerated in the past year.* Pew Research Center. https://www.pewresearch.org/short-reads/2020/11/09/the-pace-of-boomer-retirements-has-accelerated-in-the-past-year/

FTI Ontario. (2024). The Importance of Mentorship in Ontario Apprenticeships. https://ftiontario.com/the-importance-of-mentorship-in-ontario-apprenticeships/

FY 2021 data and statistics. (2021). Employment and Training Administration. https://www.dol.gov/agencies/eta/apprenticeship/about/statistics/2021

Generational communication in the workplace: Bridging the gap. (n.d.). Prospect HR Consulting. https://prospecthrc.com/communication-differences-between-generations-in-the-workplace-bridging-the-gap/

The German Vocational Training System: An Overview. (n.d.). German Missions in the United States. https://www.germany.info/us-en/welcome/wirtschaft/03-wirtschaft/1048296-1048296#:~:text=In%20Germany%2C%20more%20than%2050,companies%20participate%20in%20vocational%20training

GDP by Industry. (2025). Bea.gov. https://www.bea.gov/data/gdp/gdp-industry

Gray, K., & Herr, E. (2006). *Other ways to win: Creating alternatives for high school graduates.* Corwin Press.

Guerra, H. (2022). Will robots take your construction job? Not anytime soon. *Built.* https://blog.bluebeam.com/robots-construction-jobs/

Gwoke, R. (n.d.). *Knowledge transfer: Empowering baby boomers.* Bridgeworks. https://www.generations.com/insights/knowledge-transfer-empowering-baby-boomers

Hanson, M. (2024). *Average cost of college by year.* Education Data Initiative. https://educationdata.org/average-cost-of-college-by-year

Hill, R. (2001). *Skywalkers: Mohawk ironworkers build New York.* International Association of Bridge, Structural, Ornamental and Reinforcing Iron Workers.

Holmes, M. (2019). *Stigma in the skilled trades.* Make It Right. https://makeitright.ca/holmes-advice/mike-skilled-trades/stigma-in-the-skilled-trades

The Home Builders Institute (HBI) construction labor market report. (2024). The Home Builders Institute. https://hbi.org/wp-content/uploads/2024/09/Fall-2024-Construction-Labor-Market-Report.pdf

Horwitz, S. K., & Horwitz, I. B. (2007). The effects of team diversity on team outcomes: A meta-analytic review of team demography. *Journal of Management, 33*(6), 987-1015. https://doi.org/10.1177/0149206307308587*The future of work in construction.*

Hughes, R. (2018). Obituary: The 9/11 rescuers who died a day apart, 17 years on. *BBC*. https://www.bbc.com/news/world-us-canada-43498200

Job openings and labor turnover - February 2020. (2025). In Bureau of Labor Statistics. https://www.bls.gov/news.release/pdf/jolts.pdf

Johnston, W. (2024). Many in Gen Z ditch colleges for trade schools. Meet the 'toolbelt generation'. *NPR*. https://www.npr.org/2024/04/22/1245858737/gen-z-trade-vocational-schools-jobs-college

June 2025: EU unemployment rate at 5.9%. (2025). De Statis. https://www.destatis.de/Europa/EN/Topic/Population-Labour-Social-Issues/Labour-market/EULabourMarketCrisis.html

Izon, L. (n.d.). The importance of social media in Gen Z recruitment. *PHA*. https://thephagroup.com/blog/the-importance-of-social-media-in-gen-z-recruitment/

Labor report shows dire need for new construction workers. (2024). *National Association of Home Builders*. https://www.nahb.org/blog/2024/10/hbi-construction-labor-report-fall-2024

Knowledge sharing best practices: How to mind meld and keep everyone in the know. (n.d.). Atlassian. https://www.atlassian.com/work-management/knowledge-sharing/best-practices

Kreisman, D., & Stange, K. (2019). Depth over breadth : The value of vocational education in U.S. high schools. *Education Next, 19*(4). https://www.educationnext.org/depth-over-breadth-value-vocational-education-u-s-high-schools/

Ma, J. and Pender, M. (2023). *Trends in College Pricing and Student Aid 2023.* College Board. https://research.collegeboard.org/media/pdf/Trends%20Report%202023%20Updated.pdf

Makers index: Attitudes and awareness of the skilled trades. (2022). Stanley Black & Decker.

Manyika, J., Chui, M., Miremadi, M., Bughin, J., George, K., Willmott, P., & Dewhurst, M. (2017). *A future that works: Automation, employment, and productivity.* McKinsey Global Institute. https://www.mckinsey.com/~/media/mckinsey/featured%20insights/Digital%20Disruption/Harnessing%20automation%20for%20a%20future%20that%20works/MGI-A-future-that-works-Executive-summary.ashx

Manzo, J., Manzo, F., & Bruno, R. (2018). *The potential economic consequences of a highly automated construction industry: What if construction becomes the next manufacturing?* Midwest Economic Policy Institute. https://midwestepi.org/wp-content/uploads/2018/01/the-economic-consequences-of-a-highly-automated-construction-industry-final.pdf

Marcus, J. (2021). *Most college students don't graduate in four years, so college and the government count six years as "success".* The Hechinger Report. https://hechingerreport.org/how-the-college-lobby-got-the-government-to-measure-graduation-rates-over-six-years-instead-of-four/

Martincevic, I., & Madrigal, L. (2025). *Women in Construction Week 2025: Key statistics, expert insights, and success stories.* Fixr. https://www.fixr.com/articles/women-in-construction-week

McGriff, M. (2025). The State of women in construction in 2025. *Labor Finders.* https://www.laborfinders.com/employers/blog/women-in-construction/

Mental health and suicide prevention in construction [stats]. (2025). *Trimble.* https://www.trimble.com/blog/construction/en-US/article/mental-health-in-construction-stats

Milner, A., Page, A., & LaMontagne, A. D. (2013). Long-term unemployment and suicide: A systematic review and meta-analysis. *PLoS ONE, 8*(1).

National census of fatal occupational injuries in 2023. (2024). Bureau of Labor Statistics. https://www.bls.gov/news.release/pdf/cfoi.pdf

National Center for Education Statistics. (1994). *Vocational education in the United States: 1969-1990.* U.S. Department of Education

National Center for Education Statistics. (2015). *Career and technical education statistics.* U.S. Department of Education.

National Taskforce on Tradeswomen's Issues. (n.d.). *Recommendations of The National Taskforce on Tradeswomen's Issue for The Biden Administration Transition Team.* https://tradeswomentaskforce.org/system/files/national_taskforce_on_tradeswomens_issues_transition_memo_2.pdf

National Taskforce on Tradeswomen's Issues. (2022). *Numbers matter: Clarifying the data on women working in construction.* https://tradeswomentaskforce.org/system/files/2021_data_on_tradeswomen.docx

New York City Office of Emergency Management. (2002). *World Trade Center recovery operations final report.* NYC Archives.

Occupational outlook handbook: Construction trades. (2024). U.S. Bureau of Labor Statistics. https://www.bls.gov/ooh/construction-and-extraction/home.htm

Office of Career, Technical, and Adult Education. (n.d.). *Perkins V.* https://cte.ed.gov/legislation/perkins-v

OSHA. (2024). *Commonly used statistics in construction safety*. https://www.osha.gov

Osmond, L. J. (2025, July 15). Willis Tower. In *Britannica*. https://www.britannica.com/topic/Willis-Tower

Personal protective equipment. (2023). Occupational Safety and Health Administration. https://www.osha.gov/sites/default/files/publications/osha3151.pdf

Phillips, Z. (2024). *Construction fatalities hit highest number since 2011*. Construction Dive. https://www.constructiondive.com/news/construction-deaths-2024-safety-bls/736002/

Phillips, Z. (2025). *After 5 years, construction still reels from COVID's labor impact*. Construction Dive. https://www.constructiondive.com/news/covid-impact-construction-labor-five-years/742445/

Program impact report 2015-2024. (2024). Power Up

Raymond, D., Dreher, A. (2022). *Drilling into the Skilled Trades Shortage: Stanley Black & Decker's Inaugural Makers Index Reveals Few Students Likely to Consider a Career in the Trades; Outdated Perceptions Key Drivers*. Stanley Black&Decker. https://ir.stanleyblackanddecker.com/news-events/press-releases/news-details/2022/Drilling-into-the-Skilled-Trades-Shortage-Stanley-Black--Deckers-Inaugural-Makers-Index-Reveals-Few-Students-Likely-to-Consider-a-Career-in-the-Trades-Outdated-Perceptions-Key-Drivers/default.aspx

Robinson, K. (2015). *Why Schools Need to Bring Back Shop Class*. Time. https://time.com/3849501/why-schools-need-to-bring-back-shop-class

Richard, O. C., Triana, M. D. C., & Li, M. (2021). The effects of racial diversity congruence between upper management and lower management on firm productivity. *Academy of Management.* https://journals.aom.org/doi/abs/10.5465/amj.2019.0468?journalCode=amj

Ridderbusch, K. (2025). *Beyond hard hats: Mental struggles become the deadliest construction industry danger.* KFF Health News. https://kffhealthnews.org/news/article/construction-workers-suicide-mental-health-workplace-opioids-overdose-alabama/#:~:text=BIRMINGHAM%2C%20Ala.

Rideout, V., Peebles, A., Mann, S., & Robb, M. B. (2021). *The common sense census: Media use by tweens and teens, 2021.* Common Sense. https://www.commonsensemedia.org/sites/default/files/research/report/8-18-census-integrated-report-final-web_0.pdf

Rosenbaum, J. E. (2001). *Beyond college for all: Career paths for the forgotten half.* Russell Sage Foundation.

Rowe, M. (2023). *The way I heard it.* Gallery Books.

The Safety Sentinel. (2025). National ladder safety month. LinkedIn. https://www.linkedin.com/pulse/safety-sentinel-march-2025-naspweb-licjc/

Santana, M. C. (2016). From empowerment to domesticity: The case of Rosie the Riveter and the WWII campaign. *Frontiers in Sociology, 1.* https://doi.org/10.3389/fsoc.2016.00016

Sayantani. (2024). *9/11 terror attacks: Looking back at the '1 hour and 40 minutes' that haunts US till date.* Mint. https://www.livemint.com/news/us-news/911-terror-attack-looking-back-at-the-1-hour-and-40-minutes-that-haunts-us-al-qaeda-george-bush-barack-obama-11726059499546.html

Shortell, D., & Kounang, N. (2018). FBI official, dead of 9/11-related cancer, remembered as number of cases grows. *CNN*. https://edition.cnn.com/2018/06/18/health/9-11-fbi-cancer#:~:text=FBI%20agent%20David%20LeValley%20died

Shriber, S. (2023). *3 key social media trends among Gen Z and millennials*. Civic Science. https://civicscience.com/3-key-social-media-trends-among-gen-z-and-millennials/#:~:text=CivicScience%20data%20show%20that%2090

Shukman, D. (2011, September 1). Toxic dust legacy of 9/11 plagues thousands of people. *BBC News*. http://www.bbc.co.uk/news/world-us-canada-14738140

Smith, E. C., Holmes, L., & Burkle, F. M. (2019). The physical and mental health challenges experienced by 9/11 first responders and recovery workers: A review of the literature. Cambridge University Press. *Prehospital and Disaster Medicine, 34*(6), 625-631. doi:10.1017/S1049023X19004989

Standards of apprenticeship. (2019). *Washington State Apprenticeship and Training Council*. https://apps-public.lni.wa.gov/TradesLicensing/Apprenticeship/files/standards/2151.pdf

Stanley, A. (2023). *Baby boomers are hitting peak 65. What it means for retirement planning*. Peak 65. https://www.protectedincome.org/news/baby-boomers-are-hitting-peak-65-what-it-means-for-retirement-planning/#:~:text=And%20by%202030%2C%20all%20boomers

The state of career technical education: An analysis of states' Perkins V priorities. (2020). Advance CTE. https://cte.careertech.org/wp-content/uploads/2023/01/State_CTE_PerkinsV_2020.pdf

Stout, G., Vitchers, C., & Gray, R. (2006). *Nine months at Ground Zero: The story of the brotherhood of workers who took on a job like no other.* Scribner.

Talpur, B. D. (2025). Is automated construction on the horizon? *PAAcademy.* https://paacademy.com/blog/is-automated-construction-on-the-horizon#:~:text=According%20to%20a%20MarketsandMarketsTM%20analysis

Term enrollment estimates: Spring 2023. (2023). National Student Clearinghouse Research Center. https://nscresearchcenter.org/wp-content/uploads/CTEE_Report_Spring_2023.pdf

Torpey, E. (2024, January).Bureau of Labor Statistics.https://www.bls.gov/careeroutlook/2024/article/education-level-and-projected-openings.htm

Travelers. (n.d.). *Suicide in the construction industry.* https://www.travelers.com/resources/business-industries/construction/suicide-in-the-construction-industry#:~:text=Suicide%20and%20construction%20workers&text=Fifty%2Dsix%20out%20of%20every

Tremper, N. (2024). *Slowed hiring in white collar jobs is driving GenZ toward skilled trades.* Gusto. https://gusto.com/resources/gusto-insights/skilled-trade-workers-2024

Trump, D. J. (2025, May). [Status]. Truth Social. https://truthsocial.com/@realDonaldTrump

12 Golden Gate Bridge fun facts that just might surprise you. (n.d.). *Go Car.* https://gocartours.com/blog/golden-gate-bridge-fun-facts/

2024's percentage of women in construction: The rising stats. (2024). *ClockShark.* https://www.clockshark.com/blog/women-construction-trades.

2023 workforce survey analysis. (2023). Associated General Contractors of America & Autodesk. https://www.agc.org/sites/default/files/users/user21902/2023%20Workforce%20Survey%20Analysis%20(3).pdf

U.S. Department of Education. (1994). *National assessment of vocational education: Final report*

Van Durme, Y., Scoble-Williams, N., Eaton, K., Kirby, L., Griffiths, M., Poynton, S., Mallon, D., & Forsythe, J. (2023). *Deloitte 2023 global human capital trends: New fundamentals for a boundaryless world.* Deloitte. https://www.deloitte.com/us/en/insights/topics/talent/human-capital-trends/2023/future-of-workforce-management.html

Why job seekers rely on social media. (n.d.). Mansi Media. https://mansimedia.com/why-job-seekers-rely-on-social-media/#:~:text=Glassdoor%20reports%20that%2079%25%20of

Why weren't 9/11 recovery workers protected at the World Trade Center? Hearing before the Committee on Education and Labor, 110–62. (2007). U.S. House of Representatives One Hundred Tenth Congress, First Session. https://www.911healthwatch.org/files/CHRG-110hhrg36730.pdf

Women in construction: Still breaking ground. (2014). National Women's Law Center. https://nwlc.org/wp-content/uploads/2015/08/final_nwlc_womeninconstruction_report.pdf

Women in Construction: The State of the Industry in 2024. (2024). BigRentz. https://www.bigrentz.com/blog/women-construction#:~:text=The%20rate%20of%20women%20in,each%20year%20over%20the%20decade

Women in Construction Week™ 2025: Key Statistics, Expert Insights, and Success Stories. (2025). Fixr. https://assets.fixr.com/fixr-2025women_construction_report-1740755739.pdf

Women in the labor force: A databook. (2023). U.S. Bureau of Labor Statistics. https://www.bls.gov/opub/reports/womens-databook/2022/

World Economic Forum. (2025). *Future of Jobs Report 2025.* WEF. https://reports.weforum.org/docs/WEF_Future_of_Jobs_Report_2025.pdf

www.ingramcontent.com/pod-product-compliance
Lightning Source LLC
Chambersburg PA
CBHW060502030426
42337CB00015B/1700